SUCCESS AND LUCK

SUCCESS ♠ND LUCK

Good Fortune

and the Myth of Meritocracy

ROBERT H. FRANK

Princeton University Press
Princeton and Oxford

Requests for permission to reproduce material from this
work should be sent to Permissions, Princeton University Press
Published by Princeton University Press,
41 William Street, Princeton, New Jersey 08540
In the United Kingdom: Princeton University Press,
6 Oxford Street, Woodstock, Oxfordshire OX20 1TR
press.princeton.edu

Cover design by Will Brown

Library of Congress Cataloging-in-Publication Data

Names: Frank, Robert H., author.
Title: Success and luck : good fortune and the myth of meritocracy / Robert H.
    Frank.
Description: Princeton : Princeton University Press, [2016] | Includes
    bibliographical references and index.
Identifiers: LCCN 2015040858 | ISBN 9780691167404 (hardcover : alk. paper)
Subjects: LCSH: Economics. | Fortune—Economic aspects. | Success—Economic
    aspects. | Merit (Ethics)—Economic aspects. | Economics—Sociological aspects.
    | Economics—Psychological aspects.
Classification: LCC HB71 .F69584 2016 | DDC 650.1—dc23 LC record available at
    http://lccn.loc.gov/2015040858

British Library Cataloging-in-Publication Data is available

This book has been composed in ScalaOT

Printed on acid-free paper. ∞

Printed in the United States of America

10 9 8 7 6 5 4 3 2 1

*Luck is not something you can mention
in the presence of self-made men.*
E. B. WHITE

Fifth Philosopher's Song

A million million spermatozoa
All of them alive;
Out of their cataclysm but one poor Noah
Dare hope to survive.
And among that billion minus one
Might have chanced to be
Shakespeare, another Newton, a new Donne—
But the One was Me.
Shame to have ousted your betters thus,
Taking ark while the others remained outside!
Better for all of us, froward Homunculus,
If you'd quietly died!

—ALDOUS HUXLEY (1920)

CONTENTS

PREFACE

How important is luck? Few questions more reliably divide conservatives from liberals. As conservatives correctly observe, people who amass great fortunes are almost always extremely talented and hardworking. But as liberals also rightly note, countless others have those same qualities yet never earn much.

In recent years, social scientists have discovered that chance events play a much larger role in important life outcomes than most people once imagined. In *Success and Luck*, I explore the intriguing and sometimes unexpected implications of those findings for how best to think about the role of luck in life.

My original working subtitle for the book was "A Personal Perspective." I chose it out of concern that some readers might object if not given sufficient notice that my story includes numerous accounts of my own experiences with chance events. But my editors at Princeton persuaded me that "A Personal Perspective" could lead many to mistake the book for an autobiography, which *Success and Luck* is not. Their worry, unstated but no doubt valid, was that autobiographies of noncelebrities attract few readers.

Because I've long argued that the market systems of most developed economies are now far more meritocratic than at any time in history, I was reluctant at first to embrace Princeton's proposed alternative, "Good Fortune and the Myth of Meritocracy." My concerns were confirmed by the reaction of a longtime colleague when I showed him a mockup of the book's cover. "Why SHOULDN'T companies hire the most qualified applicants?" he asked. I assured him that I was as vehemently opposed to cronyism as he was.

As a practical matter, of course, no system could ever be perfectly meritocratic. But my eventual decision to go with "Good Fortune and the Myth of Meritocracy" had little to do with concern about whatever vestiges of cronyism and class privilege might persist. Rather, it was because I believe the rhetoric of meritocracy has caused enormous harm.

The term itself was coined in 1958 by the British sociologist (and later lord) Michael Young in a scathing satire of the British educational system. In *The Rise of the Meritocracy*, he argued that encouraging successful people to self-aggrandizingly attribute their success solely to their own efforts and abilities would actually make things worse, on balance.[1] In a 2001 column reflecting on the book, he noted that although it makes good sense to appoint people to jobs on their merit, "It is the opposite when those who are judged to have merit of a particular kind harden into a new social class without room in it for others."[2] Young was chagrined that the term he'd coined as a pejorative had been so quickly co-opted as an adjective of praise.

In societies that celebrate meritocratic individualism, saying that top earners may have enjoyed a bit of luck apparently verges on telling them that they don't really belong on top, that they aren't who they think they are. The rhetoric of meritocracy appears to have camouflaged the extent to which success and failure often hinge decisively on events completely beyond any individual's control. In his commencement address to Princeton University's 2012 graduating class, for example, Michael Lewis described the improbable chain of events that helped him become a rich and famous author:

One night I was invited to a dinner, where I sat next to the wife of a big shot at a giant Wall Street investment bank, called Salomon Brothers. She more or less forced her husband to give me a job. I knew next to nothing about Salomon Brothers. But Salomon Brothers happened to be where Wall Street was being reinvented—into the place we have all come to know and love. When I got there I was assigned, almost arbitrarily, to the very best job in which to observe the growing madness: they turned me into the house expert on derivatives. A year and a half later Salomon Brothers was handing me a check for hundreds of thousands of dollars to give advice about derivatives to professional investors.[3]

On the basis of his experiences at Salomon, Lewis published his 1989 breakout best seller describing how the new wave of Wall Street financial maneuvering was transforming the world:

The book I wrote was called *Liar's Poker*. It sold a million copies. I was 28 years old. I had a career, a little fame, a small fortune and a new life narrative. All of a sudden people were telling me I was born to be a writer. This was absurd. Even I could see there was another, truer narrative, with luck as its theme. What were the odds of being seated at that dinner next to that Salomon Brothers lady? Of landing inside the best Wall Street firm from which to write the story of an age? Of landing in the seat with the best view of the business? Of having parents who didn't disinherit me but instead sighed and said "do it if you must?" Of having had that sense of must kindled inside me by a professor of art history at Princeton? Of having been let into Princeton in the first place?

This isn't just false humility. It's false humility with a point. My case illustrates how success is always rationalized. People really don't like to hear success explained away as luck—especially successful people. As they age, and succeed, people feel their success was somehow inevitable. They don't want to acknowledge the role played by accident in their lives.

The *New York Times* columnist Nicholas Kristof has often sounded a similar theme:

> One delusion common among America's successful people is that they triumphed just because of hard work and intelligence.
>
> In fact, their big break came when they were conceived in middle-class American families who loved them, read them stories, and nurtured them with Little League sports, library cards and music lessons. They were programmed for success by the time they were zygotes.[4]

A dark side of this delusion, Kristof notes, is that those who are oblivious to their own advantages are often similarly oblivious to other people's disadvantages:

> The result is a meanspiritedness in the political world or, at best, a lack of empathy toward those struggling—partly explaining the hostility to state expansion of Medicaid, to long-term unemployment benefits, or to raising the minimum wage to keep up with inflation.

Kristof recounts the life history of Rick Goff, a friend from his small hometown in Oregon. Shortly after Goff's mother died when he was five, his alcoholic father abandoned Goff and his three siblings to raise themselves. People who knew Goff describe him as a loyal friend. He was also said to have had a "terrific mind" but did poorly in school because of an undiagnosed attention deficit disorder. He dropped out before finishing the tenth grade, then worked in lumber mills and machine shops before going on to become a talented painter of custom cars. But after seriously injuring his hand in an accident, he struggled to get by on disability payments and odd jobs. His untimely death at sixty-five in July 2015 was triggered by his inability to afford a crucial medication because he'd spent $600 to bail his ex-wife out of a financial emergency.

As Kristof concludes,

> Some think success is all about "choices" and "personal responsibility." Yes, those are real, but it's so much more complicated than that.
> "Rich kids make a lot of bad choices," [Stanford sociologist Sean] Reardon notes. "They just don't come with the same sort of consequences."[5]

Michael Lewis concluded his Princeton address by describing an experiment conducted by psychologists at the University of California at Berkeley.[6] The researchers sent volunteer subjects into small rooms in same-sex groups of three and gave them a complex moral problem to resolve, such as what to do about an episode of cheating on an exam. Arbitrarily, they assigned one member of each group as its leader. Thirty minutes into each team's deliberations, a researcher entered the room with a plate bearing four cookies for the three volunteers.

Who ate the extra cookie? In each case, it was the leader of the group, even though, as Lewis notes, "He had no special virtue.

He'd been chosen at random, 30 minutes earlier. His status was nothing but luck. But it still left him with the sense that the cookie should be his."

Lewis sketches this moral of the experiment for Princeton graduates:

> In a general sort of way you have been appointed the leader of the group. Your appointment may not be entirely arbitrary. But you must sense its arbitrary aspect: you are the lucky few. Lucky in your parents, lucky in your country, lucky that a place like Princeton exists that can take in lucky people, introduce them to other lucky people, and increase their chances of becoming even luckier. Lucky that you live in the richest society the world has ever seen, in a time when no one actually expects you to sacrifice your interests to anything.
>
> All of you have been faced with the extra cookie. All of you will be faced with many more of them. In time you will find it easy to assume that you deserve the extra cookie. For all I know, you may. But you'll be happier, and the world will be better off, if you at least pretend that you don't.

There are of course many people who are quick to acknowledge good fortune's contribution to their success. Those people, it turns out, are much more likely than others to support the kinds of public investments that created and maintained the environments that made their own success possible. They're also substantially happier than others, as Lewis conjectured. And the very fact of their gratitude itself appears to steer additional material prosperity their way.

The claims I'll defend in the pages ahead are ambitious—that successful people tend to understate luck's role in their success, making them reluctant to support the kinds of public investments without which everyone becomes less likely to succeed; and that a relatively simple, unintrusive change in public policy could free up more than enough resources to redress this investment shortfall.

My arguments in support of these claims have few moving parts, and none of the premises on which they rest is controversial. Princeton's initial reviewers offered numerous suggestions for additional topics I might address, many of them interesting. But since none was essential for my arguments, I resisted those suggestions. My aim from the outset was to produce a book that would demand no more of your time than necessary, and the one you're holding is indeed mercifully short. My deepest hope is that if my arguments resonate with you, you'll want to discuss them with others.

ACKNOWLEDGMENTS

Many people have offered useful advice and encouragement since I began thinking about this project several years ago. I especially want to thank my wife, Ellen McCollister, whose service as a member of Ithaca's city council has so forcefully reminded me and others in our community that good government is possible. In contrast to many of my economics colleagues, I spend almost no time trying to prove mathematical theorems and a great deal of time thinking about the experiences of real people. Not least among the attractions of that time allocation has been the opportunity it's given me to discuss issues with Ellen and to benefit from her rich insights about human psychology.

Others too numerous to mention have also been enormously helpful. With apologies to those I neglect to mention explicitly, I'd like to express my sincere gratitude to Peter Bloom, Summer Brown, Bruce Buchanan, CAU seminar participants, Philip Cook, Richard Dawkins, David DeSteno, Nick Epley, Alissa Fishbane, Chris Frank, David Frank, Hayden Frank, Jason Frank, Srinagesh Gavernini, Tom Gilovich, Piper Goodeve, Janet Greenfield, Jon Haidt, Ori Heffetz, Yuezhou Hou, Graham Kerslick, Kathi Mestayer, Dave Nussbaum, NYU Paduano Seminar participants, Sam Pizzigati, Dennis Regan, Russell Sage Foundation seminar participants, Kirsten Saracini, Eric Schoenberg, Barry Schwartz, Larry Seidman, Amit Singh, Rory Sutherland, David Sloan Wilson, Andrew Wylie, and Caitlin

Zaloom for their advice and encouragement. They of course bear no responsibility for any remaining errors. I'm also grateful to Honor Jones and Kathleen Kageff for their skillful editorial assistance. And finally, I thank Peter Dougherty and Seth Ditchik at Princeton University Press for their enthusiastic support and, above all, for their enduring faith that books still matter.

1
♠

WRITE WHAT YOU KNOW

Writers are told to "write what you know," and that's one reason I began writing about luck several years ago. I became interested in the subject in part because chance events have figured so prominently in my own life.

Perhaps the most extreme example occurred on a chilly November Saturday morning in 2007, when I was playing tennis at an indoor facility with my longtime friend and collaborator, the Cornell psychologist Tom Gilovich. He later told me that as we sat between games early in the second set, I complained of feeling nauseated. The next thing he knew, I was lying motionless on the court.

When he kneeled to investigate, he discovered that I wasn't breathing and had no pulse. He yelled out for someone to call 911, then flipped me onto my back and started pounding on my chest—something he'd seen many times in movies but had never been trained to do. He says that after what seemed like forever, he got a cough out of me. Shortly after that an ambulance showed up.

Since ambulances are dispatched from the other side of town, more than five miles away, how did this one arrive so quickly?

By happenstance, about half an hour before I collapsed, two ambulances had been dispatched to two separate auto accidents that had occurred close to the tennis center. Since the injuries involved in one of them weren't serious, one of the drivers was able to peel off and travel just a few hundred yards to get to me. The EMTs put the paddles on me, then rushed me to our local hospital. There I was loaded onto a helicopter and flown to a larger hospital in Pennsylvania, where they put me on ice overnight.

Doctors later told me that I'd suffered an episode of sudden cardiac death. They said that 98 percent of those who experience such episodes don't survive them and that most of the few who do are left with significant cognitive and other impairments. And for three days after the event, my family tells me, I spoke nonstop gibberish from my hospital bed. But by day four I was discharged with a clear head. Two weeks later, after having passed the first cardiac stress test my doctors could schedule, I was playing tennis with Tom again.

If an extra ambulance hadn't happened to be nearby, I would not have survived. Some friends have suggested that I was the beneficiary of divine intervention, and I have no quarrel with those who see things that way. But that's never been a comfortable view for me. I believe I'm alive today because of pure dumb luck.

Not all chance events lead to favorable outcomes, of course. Mike Edwards is no longer alive simply because chance frowned on him. He was the cellist in the original group that became the Electric Light Orchestra, the British pop band. He was driving on a rural road in England in 2010 when a thirteen-hundred-pound bale of hay rolled down a steep hillside and landed on top of his van, crushing him to death. He hadn't broken any laws that day. By all accounts, he was a well-liked, decent, and peaceful man. That his life was snuffed out by a runaway bale of hay was just bad luck, pure and simple.

Most people have no difficulty embracing the view that I'm lucky to have survived and that Edwards was unlucky to have perished. But in other domains, randomness often plays out in far more subtle ways, causing many of those same people to resist explanations that invoke luck. In particular, many seem uncomfortable with the possibility that success in the marketplace depends to any significant extent on luck.

A few years back I wrote a newspaper column describing how seemingly minor chance events figure much more prominently in life trajectories than most people realize.[1] It was the first in a series of pieces I wrote that have gradually evolved into this book. I was surprised by the intense negative commentary the column generated, most of it from people who insisted that success is explained almost entirely by talent and effort. Those qualities are indeed highly important. But because the contests that mete out society's biggest prizes are so bitterly competitive, talent and effort alone are rarely enough to ensure victory. In almost every case, a substantial measure of luck is also necessary.

A few days after the column appeared, I was invited to appear on a Fox Business News show hosted by Stuart Varney, a man deeply skeptical about the importance of luck. Ever the optimist, I agreed, hoping that he and his viewers might find food for thought in the evidence I would describe.

Wrong. From start to finish during the segment, Varney was in high dudgeon.[2] "Professor, wait a minute, do you know how insulting that was when I read that? I came to America with nothing thirty-five years ago. I've made something of myself, I think, with nothing but talent, hard work and risk taking. And you're going to write in the *New York Times* that this is luck?"

I tried to explain that that had not in fact been my message— that I'd written that although success is extremely difficult to achieve without talent and hard work, there are nonetheless many highly talented and hardworking people who never achieve any significant material success. But Varney's anger persisted. Spittle collecting at the corners of his mouth, he shouted, "You're saying that the American dream isn't really the American dream, it's not really there!" I tried to explain that I wasn't saying any such thing.

Varney: "Am I lucky being who I am and where I am?"

Me: "Yes! And so am I!"

Varney: "That's outrageous! Do you know what risk is involved coming to America with absolutely nothing? Do you know what risk is involved trying to work for a major American network with a British accent? A total foreigner? Do you know what risk is implied for this level of success?"

And on it went, for more than six excruciating minutes. It was only in my taxi leaving the studio that I realized all the easy rejoinders I'd failed to deliver. Varney came to America with nothing? Nonsense! I'd read the night before that he has a degree from the London School of Economics, which has always been a formidable credential in the American labor market.

Handicapped by a British accent? Oh, please! Americans *love* British accents! The British geologist Frank H. T. Rhodes became Cornell University's president shortly after I started teaching here in the 1970s. A friend once told me that Rhodes's Oxbridge accent was much stronger during his later years at Cornell than when he'd first arrived in the United States decades earlier. Certain other accents are socially disadvantageous, of course, and linguists have discovered that those tend to decay over time. But not the British accent.

Varney took risks! If I hadn't realized it on my own during my cab ride from the studio, the implication of that remark would have been hammered home to me by several e-mail messages I received later that day from friends. Taking a risk means that a successful outcome isn't certain. So if Varney took risks and was successful, he was lucky by definition! Too bad I didn't have the wit to point that out during our conversation on the air.

I've often wished I had the talent for thinking on my feet displayed by the protagonists in the novels of Elmore Leonard, long my favorite fiction author. Shortly after he died in 2013, NPR's Terry Gross aired excerpts from two of her earlier interviews with him.[3] At one point she mentioned the uncanny verbal dexterity of his characters. In real life, she asked, can Leonard himself match their ability to deliver such snappy comeback lines?

He demurred: "Oh no … never …" It's different in writing, he explained: "… you end the scene with a line, the perfect line … you have months to think about it."

Gross pressed him, wanting to know whether he mulled over his own conversations after the fact, trying to come up with clever replies he wished he'd thought of. And without missing a beat, Leonard offered this:

"Well, in real life, I'm sitting on a bench in Aspen, 4:00 in the afternoon, dead tired, I've come down the mountain, and a woman skis down, twenty-five, thirty years younger than I am, puts one boot up on the bench and says, 'I don't know what's more satisfying, taking off my boots or …' and then she used an expression for sleeping with somebody."

Gross: "And you said … ??"

Leonard: "And I said, 'huh,' … 'er,' … 'ehh' … and that was probably fifteen years ago," adding that he'd been trying ever since that day, without success, to come up with even a decent comeback line, never mind a snappy one.

It's hard to imagine a more pitch-perfect response to Gross's query. Did they rehearse that exchange? It didn't sound like it, and if not, it suggests that Leonard was actually pretty good at thinking on his feet. It's a talent I often lack. Most of the time, as in my conversation with Stuart Varney, the cost has been only some fleeting embarrassment. But occasionally it's been painful, and on one occasion, I was lucky to escape with my life.

I was windsurfing on Cayuga Lake on an extremely gusty afternoon, winds ranging from dead calm to more than forty miles an hour. To make it easier to hold the mast and sail upright in heavy wind, many windsurfers use a harness, which is just a life jacket with a hook in front that attaches to a loop of rope tied to the boom. (This apparatus lets the windsurfer's body weight do much of the work, relieving fatigue in the hands and arms.) After a brief lull, an especially strong gust blew through, catapulting me over the boom and sail. The next thing I knew, I was submerged under the sail, dazed but still conscious. As my head cleared, my first impulse was to release the hook from the rope so I could swim out from under the sail. But since my body had done several twists before hitting the water, the rope was wrapped too tightly around the hook for me to break free.

So I went to plan B, which was to push up hard on the sail above me, hoping to create some airspace between it and the lake surface. No progress with that, either, so I tried again to get the hook free from the rope. Again, no progress.

In full panic by this time and desperate for air, I made another futile attempt at the sail, then tried once more to disengage the hook. Again, failure. Hope fading, I tried the sail one more time. And that last effort produced a glorious sucking sound as air rushed up beneath it. I rose to the surface and breathed deeply for a few moments.

Once I calmed down, I saw what I should have seen right away: It wasn't necessary to free the hook from the rope. Simply by unzipping my life vest and removing it, I could have swum out from under the submerged sail. That's of course what I did, in the end. But not before almost drowning. Survival is sometimes just a matter of pure dumb luck, and I was clearly luck's beneficiary that day.

Stuart Varney and many others insist that people who amass great fortunes are invariably talented, hardworking, and socially productive. That's a bit of an overstatement—think of lip-synching boy bands, or derivatives traders who got spectacularly rich before bringing the world economy to its knees. Yet it's clear that most of the biggest winners in the marketplace are both extremely talented and hardworking. On this point, Varney is largely correct.

But what about the many talented and hardworking people who never achieve much material success? I often think of Birkhaman Rai, the young hill tribesman from Bhutan who was my cook long ago when I was a Peace Corps volunteer in a small village in Nepal. To this day, he remains perhaps the most enterprising and talented person I've ever met. He could thatch a roof and repair an alarm clock. A skilled cook, he could also resole shoes. He could plaster a wall, after having made the plaster himself from cow dung, mud, and other free ingredients. He could butcher a goat. He could bargain tough with local merchants without alienating them.

Though he'd never been taught to read and write, there was almost no practical task in that environment that he couldn't perform to a high standard. Even so, the meager salary I was able to pay him was almost certainly the high point of his life's earnings trajectory. If he'd grown up in the United States or some other rich country, he would have been far more prosperous, perhaps even spectacularly successful. As the economist Branko Milanovic has estimated, roughly half of the variance in incomes across persons worldwide is explained by only two factors: country of residence and the income distribution within that country.[4] As Napoleon Bonaparte once observed, "Ability is of little account without opportunity."

But if talent and hard work don't guarantee material success, I hope we can all agree that success is much more likely for people with talents that are highly valued by others, and also for those with the ability and inclination to focus intently and work tirelessly. But where do those personal qualities come from? We don't know, precisely, other than to say that they spring from some combination of genes and the environment (although recent work by biologists suggests that there may be important random influences here as well).[5]

In some unknown proportion, genetic and environmental factors largely explain whether someone gets up in the morning feeling eager to begin work. If you're such a person, which much of the time I am not, you're fortunate. Similarly, your genes and your environment largely determine how smart you are. If you're smart, you're more likely to perform well at the tasks rewarded most lavishly by society, so there, too, you're lucky. As the economist Alan Krueger has noted, the correlation between parents' income and their children's income in the United States is a remarkably high 0.5—about the same as the correlation between parents' height and their children's height.[6] So if you want to be smart and highly energetic, the most important single step you could take is to choose the right parents. But if you have such qualities, on what theory would it make sense for you to claim moral credit for them? You didn't choose your parents, nor did you have much control over the environment in which you were raised. You were just lucky.

Many people don't like to work hard and also have limited endowments of cognitive abilities and other traits that are highly valued in the marketplace. In the competitive environments most of us inhabit, those people are unlucky.

In short, even if talent and hard work alone were enough to ensure material success—which they are not—luck would remain an essential part of the story. People with a lot of talent and an inclination to work hard are extremely fortunate.

But luck's role in explaining differences in personal attributes is not my focus here. Instead, I want to describe what researchers have learned in recent years about the influence of external chance events and environmental factors on important individual life outcomes—influences that occur independently of people's virtues or flaws.

Having cheated death on at least two occasions obviously does not, by itself, make me an authority on luck. But it has instilled in me a keen interest in the subject and has stimulated me to learn much more about it than I otherwise would have. My personal experiences with chance events in the labor market have also spurred me to learn more about how such events shape career trajectories.

The influence of even seemingly minor random events is often profound. Is the *Mona Lisa* special? Is Kim Kardashian? They're both famous, but sometimes things are famous just for being famous. Although we often try to explain their success by scrutinizing their objective qualities, they are in fact often no more special than many of their less renowned counterparts.

Ahead I'll describe how success often results from positive feedback loops that amplify tiny initial variations into enormous differences in final outcomes. I'll also describe several individual case histories illustrating how even the most spectacular success stories could easily have unfolded very differently.

Chance events have always mattered, of course, but in some respects they've grown more important in recent decades. One reason for that has been the spread and intensification of what the economist Philip Cook and I have called winner-take-all markets.[7] These markets often arise when technology enables the most gifted performers in an arena to extend their reach. Tax advice, for example, was once a quintessentially local undertaking. The best accountants in a town served the biggest clients, the next-best served the next biggest, and so on. But the development of user-friendly tax software transformed this market into one in which the most able practitioners can serve almost everyone.

Scores of competing tax programs battled for supremacy in the early years. But once reviewers reached consensus on which ones were best, rival programs became redundant, because it was possible to reproduce copies of the best programs at essentially zero cost. In the end, Intuit's *Turbo Tax* captured almost the entire market. Its developers profited enormously, even as those whose programs were almost as good were being forced out of business. In such markets, the quality difference between best and second best is often barely perceptible, but the corresponding difference in rewards can be enormous.

Technology has been creating similar winner-take-all markets in other domains, including law, medicine, sports, journalism, retail, manufacturing, even academia. In these and many other arenas, new methods of production and communication have amplified the effect of chance events, greatly magnifying the gaps between winners and losers. It's one thing to say that someone who works 1 percent harder than others or is 1 percent more talented deserves 1 percent more income. But the importance of chance looms much larger when such small performance differences translate into thousands-fold differences in earnings.

The spread of winner-take-all markets has amplified the importance of chance in a second way. In almost all cases, the prodigious rewards that accrue to a handful of winners in these markets attract enormous numbers of contestants. And the more contestants there are, the more luck matters.

Consider a contest that is completely meritocratic in the sense of being settled on the basis of objective performance alone, and suppose that 98 percent of each contestant's performance is accounted for by talent and effort, only 2 percent by luck. Given these weights, it's clear that no one could win without being both highly talented and hardworking. But less obvious, perhaps, is that the winner is also likely to have been among the luckiest of all contestants. Luck matters so much in contests like these because winning requires that almost everything go right. There will inevitably be many contestants close to the top of the talent and effort scale, and at least some of them are bound to have been lucky as well. So even when luck has only a minor influence on performance, the most talented and hardworking of all contestants will usually be outdone by a rival who is almost as talented and hardworking but also considerably luckier. As we'll see, if we simulated the outcome of this specific contest a thousand times, only a small minority of winners would have higher combined skill and effort levels than all other contestants.

Why do so many of us downplay luck in the face of compelling evidence of its importance? The tendency may owe in part to the fact that by emphasizing talent and hard work to the exclusion of other factors, successful people reinforce their claim to the money they've earned. But I'll also consider a second possibility, which is that denying the importance of luck may actually help people surmount the many obstacles that litter almost every path to success.

Perhaps the most important such obstacle is that most of us find it harder to summon effort when the resulting rewards are either delayed or uncertain. Narratives that stress luck's importance call attention to the fact that not even the most diligent current efforts can guarantee future success and by so doing may encourage some to sit back and hope for the best.

Another interesting quirk of human nature suggests a second way in which false beliefs may help people summon effort. Surveys reveal that many more than half of us believe ourselves to be in the top half of any given talent distribution, implying correspondingly unrealistic optimism about our prospects of winning any contest we enter. More realistic beliefs could thus discourage effort by leading many to conclude that their odds of success were lower than they thought.

In short, people who believe that success depends only on talent and effort and have an exaggerated sense of how talented they are may find it easier to muster the kinds of effort necessary for success. If so, those false beliefs may be perversely adaptive.

But underestimating the importance of external forces in individual success stories may also entail significant costs. It may, for example, encourage people to compete in arenas in which they have no realistic prospect of succeeding. More troubling, it also appears to make successful people more reluctant to underwrite the investments necessary to sustain environments that support material success.

As Warren Buffett once said, "Someone is sitting in the shade today because someone planted a tree a long time ago." Echoing Buffett's thought, Massachusetts senator Elizabeth Warren reminded audiences during her 2012 campaign that Americans are truly fortunate to have been born in a wealthy country with highly developed legal, educational, and other infrastructure. As she put it,

> There is nobody in this country who got rich on his own. You built a factory out there, good for you.... You moved your goods to market on the roads the rest of us paid for. You hired workers the rest of us paid to educate. You were safe in your factory because of police and firefighters that the rest of us paid for.... You built a factory and it turned into a great idea, God bless—keep a big hunk of it. But part of the underlying social contract is that you take part of that and pay it forward for the next kid who comes along.[8]

The YouTube video of her remarks that day quickly went viral, with many commentators bitterly denouncing her failure to recognize that most successful entrepreneurs had made it essentially on their own.

On reflection, however, it's difficult to dispute Senator Warren's claim that being born in a good environment is an enormous stroke of good fortune.[9] More important, it is the one form of good luck over which societies have any significant degree of control.

But that control requires high levels of investment, which many societies have lately been reluctant to support.

Proposals to increase public investment fall largely on deaf ears these days, because people see no politically realistic way to raise the necessary money. But coming up with the resources we need would be far easier than most people realize. My most compelling motivation for writing this book has in fact been my belief that we've failed to take advantage of what I'll call the mother of all possible lucky breaks: By adopting a simple change in tax policy, we could alter our spending patterns in ways that would eliminate many trillions of dollars of waste each year. A better understanding of the connection between success and luck would help us seize this opportunity.

That such an opportunity continues to exist is a direct consequence of our failure to appreciate how profoundly our choices are shaped by frames of reference. How big, for example, should a house be? How much should a wedding cost? Orthodox economic theories assume, preposterously, that our answers are completely context-free. Yet all available evidence indicates that people find it impossible even to think about such questions without a suitable frame of reference.

Few behavioral scientists would deny that our surroundings shape what we feel we need. But the profound implications of that simple fact have largely escaped the attention of economists and have not yet been fully grasped by behavioral scientists in other disciplines. If those implications are any clearer to me, it's only because having lived for two years in one of the world's poorest countries led me to focus so intently on these "framing effects" during the ensuing decades.

Sticking with my write-what-you-know theme, the most striking lesson of my experience in Nepal was that despite the dramatically lower material living standards there, my experience of day-to-day life was astonishingly similar to what I'd been used to. When I write, for example, that the same two-room house with no plumbing or electricity that seemed completely satisfactory to me there would seem shamefully inadequate in any American middle-class neighborhood, I'm merely writing what I know.

I don't mean to romanticize poverty. Many good things happen when a country's income grows, not least among them that people's children are much less likely to die before reaching adulthood. Air and water get cleaner, schools get better, roads get safer. My point is only that the standards that define "adequate" in many domains of consumption are highly elastic. When everyone spends less, those standards adjust accordingly.

Wealthy Americans have been building bigger mansions simply because they've received most of the country's recent income gains. Yet there's no evidence that, beyond a certain point, bigger houses make people any happier. Once houses reach a certain size, further across-the-board increases in square-footage merely shift the frame of reference that defines adequate. Similarly, the fact that the average American wedding now costs more than \$30,000,[10] almost three times as much as in 1980, doesn't appear to have made today's marrying couples any happier. According to one recent study, however, it appears to have made them more likely to divorce.[11] The economists Andrew Francis and Hugo Mialon estimated, for example, that couples who spent more than $20,000 on their weddings were more than 12 percent more likely to divorce during any given year than were those who spent between $5,000 and $10,000.

Framing effects have spawned waste in a second way by creating a powerful bias in favor of private consumption over public investment. The basic idea is captured in a simple example involving cars and highways.

Everyone agrees that cars would be of little use without roads and that roads would be of little use without cars. What's harder is to identify the best mix of the two categories. It's fairly easy, however, to see that the current mix in the United States is far from optimal, at least from the perspective of wealthy drivers. Consider this thought experiment: Which experience would a wealthy car enthusiast prefer: driving a Porsche 911 Turbo (purchase price, $150,000) on smooth, well-maintained highways, or driving a Ferrari F12 Berlinetta (purchase price, $333,000) on roads riddled with foot-deep potholes?

It's an easy question. Although some car buffs might quibble, I'll assume for the sake of argument that the Ferrari would be judged the better car if both could be driven on good roads.

Porsche 911 Turbo, $150,000.   Ferrari F12 Berlinetta, $333,000.

But it wouldn't be much better, since the $150,000 Porsche already has most of the design features that affect performance significantly. The economist's law of diminishing returns operates here with a vengeance. Beyond a certain point, it reminds us, the cost of achieving additional quality improvements rises very steeply. So if the Ferrari enjoys an edge, it's at most a tiny one. How, then, could anyone argue with a straight face that it would be more pleasing to drive the Ferrari on pothole-ridden roads than to drive the Porsche on well-maintained ones?

Yet, among the superwealthy, the actual quality mix of cars and highways in the United States more closely resembles Ferraris on potholes than Porsches on smooth asphalt. That's puzzling, since the latter combination could be achieved at much lower total expense. This distortion occurs because what happens when any one person spends less on a car is very different from what happens when everyone spends less. In the former case, the buyer feels deprived. But when everyone spends less, the relevant frame of reference shifts, leaving drivers just as satisfied as before.

Paradoxically, then, many societies are lucky precisely because their current consumption patterns are so wasteful. It's lucky to be wasteful because the mere existence of waste always implies opportunities to make everyone better off.

In economic terms, a situation is wasteful if it would be possible to rearrange things so that some people could better achieve their goals without requiring anyone else to settle for less. How could any rational person oppose doing something like that?

In principle, at least, there should be no political goal more easily achieved than agreeing on proposals to eliminate waste. This is a simple point, really, yet the central idea behind it is apparently not widely understood. Economists often use the expression "economic pie" to describe the total value of all resources available for pursuing our goals, so any step that reduces waste would be said to make the economic pie larger.

And simple geometry tells us that when a pie grows larger, it must be possible to divide it so that each person gets a larger slice than before. But that's just another way of saying that eliminating waste can always enable people to pursue their goals more fully. The rich can do better, and so can the poor. Conservatives can do better, and so can liberals. Blacks can do better, and so can whites.

The incentives that have created the wasteful spending patterns I'll describe are neither mysterious nor complex. Once we understand them, I will argue, it becomes a relatively simple matter to modify them.

In short, we confront a golden opportunity: A few simple policy changes would enable us to steer trillions of dollars of additional resources into desperately needed public investment without demanding painful sacrifices from anyone. On its face, that claim should strike you as preposterous. If so, you'll be surprised to see that it rests on only a few simple premises, none of which is controversial.

But that doesn't mean that implementing the required changes will be easy in practice. The opportunity we face is not one that can be seized by individuals acting alone. We must act collectively. That's a challenge because the current political climate is more sharply polarized than at any point in recent history. Proposals to restore decaying infrastructure can expect to meet stiff resistance, even from those who agree in the abstract that it must be done.

Some of that resistance springs from experiences that have led many to question the efficacy of government. Perhaps the most compellingly popular metaphor for ineffective government is the Department of Motor Vehicles, where long waits and imperious service are the stuff of legend. An Ohio blogger, for example, offered this description of a visit to a rural DMV shortly after he'd moved to the state:

> It was an old stone building, very small, with just one woman working there. I walked in, and not seeing anybody else, didn't bother with the plastic "take a number" cards and went right up to the counter. The woman glared at me and said sternly, "TAKE A NUMBER." I looked around, smiled at the absurdity, then took a number and sat down on the old wooden bench. There was nobody else in the room besides her and me. As soon as I sat down, she called out "ONE!" I said, "Hey, that's me!" and put my number back on the peg, and returned to the counter.[12]

Although it's no mystery that such experiences often spawn jaundiced views about government, the fact remains that no society can prosper without effective means for its citizens to act collectively. Without government, how could we defend ourselves, or enforce property rights, or curb pollution, or build and maintain the public infrastructure that makes us realize how lucky we were to be born here rather than in a desperately poor country?

Since government is unavoidable, it's surely worth thinking about ways to make it better. Some societies have demonstrably more effective governments than others, after all, and some of our own government institutions function much better than others.

The possibility of creating more effective government institutions is clearly demonstrated by the striking contrast between the DMV I dealt with when I first moved to Ithaca in the 1970s and the one that serves us today. The earlier version served up the same bureaucratic ineptitude described by the Ohio blogger, but today's version is completely different.

A few years ago, I sold my car to an out-of-town buyer who said that he was excited to complete the transaction except for the fact that doing so would necessitate a visit to his local DMV. I urged him to register the car in Ithaca, saying he'd be in for a pleasant surprise. He reluctantly agreed, and much to his astonishment, we were out the door with his plates in less than fifteen minutes. The transaction would have been even quicker if he hadn't made several errors in filling out his forms, which a cheerful clerk patiently helped him to correct.

What caused this transformation? Curious to find out, I spoke with Aurora Valenti, the Tompkins County clerk who'd been in charge of our local DMV for more than two decades before her recent retirement. When she first took office, she told me, employee morale was low, and customer complaints were both bitter and frequent.

One problem was that people had to wait in a long line to process their forms, then queue up a second time to pay their fees. Ms. Valenti solved that problem by persuading state officials in Albany to provide terminals that could handle both tasks. Consumers now wait in only a single line.

Her second major initiative was to put clerks through a heavy dose of sensitivity training, telling them, "Most customers would rather have a root canal than visit the DMV, and that's making both you and them unhappy." Her aim was to empower clerks to tell customers quickly and cheerfully that there were simply no problems they couldn't solve.

The turnaround has been dramatic, and morale among employees now seems high. When I told the clerk who helped the buyer of my car why I'd suggested coming to the Ithaca office, she blushed with pride, saying that she and her colleagues really enjoy their jobs.

Annual surveys by Transparency International, a nonprofit group based in Berlin, provide further evidence of the possibility of good government. Those surveys consistently place the same nations—New Zealand, the Netherlands, Switzerland, Canada, and the Scandinavian countries among them—atop the list of countries whose citizens think most highly of their governments. Few people in those countries view their government officials as corrupt, and most are satisfied with the quality of public services paid for by their taxes.

I stress the possibility of effective government in the hope of encouraging skeptics to keep an open mind about my claim that we could easily bequeath a much better society to our children. To accomplish that goal, the steps we need to take are not intrusive, nor do they require additional layers of bureaucracy. But we'll be unlikely to take those steps if too many people feel certain they can't work.

2
♠

WHY SEEMINGLY TRIVIAL
RANDOM EVENTS MATTER

Psychologists use the term "hindsight bias" to describe the human tendency to think that events are more predictable than they are. In the late 1940s, the sociologist Paul Lazarsfeld staged a vivid demonstration of the phenomenon by describing a study purporting to have found that World War II soldiers from rural areas were much better able than their urban counterparts to cope with the demands of military life.[1] Just as Lazarsfeld suspected, people who read the results of this study found them completely unsurprising: Of course the grueling lives led by rural men would make them much better equipped to endure wartime stresses! Why would anyone need to do a study to confirm that?

The twist was that the study Lazarsfeld described was a complete fabrication. The actual study found the reverse: It was the soldiers from urban areas who fared much better in the military. Lazarsfeld's point was that when you think you already know what happened, it's easy to invent reasons for why it *had* to happen.

Extending Lazarsfeld's work, the sociologist Duncan Watts has argued that hindsight bias operates with particular force when people observe unusually successful outcomes.[2] The problem, he suggested, is that it's almost always easy to create a narrative after the fact that portrays such outcomes as having been inevitable. Yet every event is the outcome of a complex and interwoven sequence of steps, each of which depends on those preceding it. If any of those earlier steps had been different, the entire trajectory would almost surely be different, too.

Watts illustrates his point with the interesting history of the *Mona Lisa*, easily the most famous painting in the world. During a visit to the Louvre, he noticed the ubiquitous throngs jostling for a closer look at the painting, even as several other canvases by Leonardo da Vinci from the same era went almost completely ignored in an adjacent gallery. To Watts, the *Mona Lisa* seemed no better than those other paintings. Curious, he did a little digging and discovered that it had languished in obscurity for most of its early life. What pushed the painting into the spotlight was apparently its theft in 1911 by Vincenzo Peruggia, an Italian maintenance worker at the Louvre who tucked it under his smock before leaving work one evening.

The theft, which was widely publicized, remained unsolved until Peruggia was apprehended two years later for attempting to sell the painting to the Uffizi Gallery in Florence. In Ian Leslie's account of the episode,

> The French public was electrified. The Italians hailed Peruggia as a patriot who wanted to return the painting home. Newspapers around the world reproduced it, making it the first work of art to achieve global fame. From then on, the "Mona Lisa" came to represent Western culture itself.[3]

As Watts writes, "We claim to be saying that the Mona Lisa is the most famous painting in the world because it has attributes X, Y and Z. But really what we're saying is that the Mona Lisa is famous because it's more like the Mona Lisa than anything else."[4]

Consider also the career of Al Pacino, one of the most celebrated actors of the past forty years. Fans may find it difficult to imagine an alternative version of history in which he did not succeed as an actor. Yet his storied career owes much to one highly improbable early casting decision.[5]

Studio executives at Paramount wanted to cast Robert Redford, Warren Beatty, or Ryan O'Neal to play Michael Corleone in Francis Ford Coppola's film adaptation of Mario Puzo's *The Godfather*. Coppola, however, wanted an unknown actor, someone who actually looked like a Sicilian. Executives remained skeptical and at one point were on the verge of signing James Caan for the role. They backed down only when Coppola threatened to abandon the project. In the end, they cast Caan as Michael's older brother Sonny and gave Pacino the starring role.

In Puzo's novel, Vito Corleone was the central character. But Vito's youngest son Michael is clearly the protagonist in Coppola's adaptation. Pacino, who had previously appeared in only two minor films, thus landed what turned out to be the most important role in what many critics have called the best film ever made. The unlikelihood of such a casting decision is underscored by the fact that Coppola was directing his first film at the age of thirty-three. Inexperienced directors almost never get their way in disputes with studio bosses.

Pacino's subsequent career affirmed the wisdom of Coppola's judgment. Those who believe that talent and hard work inevitably triumph might argue that because Pacino was relatively young at the time, his skills would have eventually made him successful even if he hadn't landed the Michael Corleone role. Maybe so. But there are also many thousands of highly talented actors who just never got the right opportunity to demonstrate their skill.

Bryan Cranston, for example, was a middle-aged supporting actor when the producer Vince Gilligan proposed casting him in the leading role of his upcoming TV series, *Breaking Bad*. Once again, studio executives were reluctant to invest so heavily in an actor who had never been cast in a major dramatic lead role. So they offered the Walter White role to John Cusack. And when Cusack turned them down, they tapped Matthew Broderick, who also declined. Gilligan again pressed his case that Cranston would be right for the part, and executives finally relented.[6]

Breaking Bad went on to become one of the most successful TV drama series of all time, in no small part because of Cranston's riveting portrayal of the ailing high school chemistry teacher turned meth kingpin. Cranston earned four Emmy Awards during the show's five seasons and is now one of the most highly sought-after actors in the profession. He's a gifted performer, to be sure, but there are thousands of other gifted performers who continue to labor out of the limelight. It seems safe to say that Cranston would not have become a superstar if either Cusack or Broderick had taken the Walter White role.

Career trajectories in acting offer some of the clearest illustrations of the positive-feedback process known as the Matthew Effect, after the verse in the book of Matthew that reads, "For unto everyone that hath shall be given, and he shall have abundance; but from him that hath not shall be taken away even that which he hath." The term was coined by the sociologist Robert K. Merton to describe how the ripple effects of seemingly minor events often profoundly alter the careers of scientific researchers.[7]

The Matthew Effect also applies in economics. As American PhD students in economics near the completion of their studies, most look for jobs at the annual meetings of the American Economic Association. Those meetings were in New Orleans when I was a fourth-year Berkeley PhD student in the job market in 1971. By the time I boarded my plane in San Francisco on a dreary late-December morning, the virus that had been stalking me for several days had developed into a full-blown case of flu. Bad luck.

I struggled through my interviews with a 104° temperature, almost certainly making an unfavorable impression at every turn. I left New Orleans in a funk, thinking nobody of sound mind would want to interview me further. To my surprise, however, I got three callbacks. Cornell invited me to travel east for a campus visit, as did the University of Wisconsin and a lesser-known school in the Midwest.

The unnamed school was my first trip. At the time, it was an institution that emphasized teaching over research, so it would not have been an ideal destination for a research-oriented economist like me. I knew my options were likely to be limited, though, so I gave the best talk I could. It was apparently good enough, since the department chair called to offer me a job several days later.

Relieved that I wasn't going to strike out completely, I then went to Cornell, and several days after my talk there, I received my second offer. When I asked whether I could let them know after my Wisconsin trip ten days hence, they said no—that their offer would expire in five days. I accepted on the spot. The Cornell economics department was nearly as good as Wisconsin's, and since it was far from certain that Wisconsin would offer me a job, it was an easy decision.

Shortly after I arrived on campus the next year, a young professor who'd been involved in my hiring told me that the seven new professors that Cornell's economics department had just brought on were several more than it had hired in any previous year. He also told me that I'd been the seventh hire. Sotto voce, he added that when he had seconded the motion that I receive an offer, the department chairman was so angered that he threw a piece of chalk at him from across the room. (A volatile man, he apparently favored some other candidate.) Suffice it to say that I got the job by the skin of my teeth. And that means I almost certainly wouldn't have gotten an offer from Wisconsin.

Bottom line: I got lucky. If not for an exceptionally unlikely confluence of events, the outcome of my job search that year would have been to end up at a teaching institution in the Midwest. As it turns out, one of my graduate school classmates was hired by that very same school. Over the years, he would call me from time to time, just wanting to talk, complaining that few of his colleagues were doing anything he found interesting. He would occasionally describe animated discussions with smart undergraduates about term papers they'd written, but most of the time he found little stimulus in his environment. Expectations about faculty research were low. I know that if I'd gone there, I would have fit right in. I'm a lazy procrastinator by nature, and if my supervisors hadn't expected me to produce much, I could have delivered on that. But by a stroke of good fortune I ended up at Cornell, which turned out to be a magnificent environment for me.

My getting tenure at Cornell was even less likely than having been hired here in the first place. In my second year, I went through a difficult marriage breakup. (Is there any other kind?) I was the primary caregiver for our two young sons during the next several years, which meant having to leave my office every day before 3:00. I was able to do very little writing and by the end of my third year had only a single published paper, one that I'd written jointly with a classmate during graduate school. My PhD thesis contained little of interest, and I had essentially nothing else in the pipeline.

Edward M. Gramlich, 1939–2007.
Photo: Gerald R. Ford School of Public Policy, University of Michigan.

These days, assistant professors with records like that almost always get fired during their third-year review. But standards were a little looser then, and since I was doing well in the classroom and didn't cost much, the department renewed my contract for another three years. It would be a gross understatement, however, to say that my prospects for being able to stay beyond that were bleak.

During my fourth year, Ned Gramlich, an accomplished policy economist, came to the department as a visiting faculty member.[8] He and I quickly became friends, often spending winter Saturdays skiing with our children. We had stimulating conversations about economics on the ski lifts. None of my senior colleagues had taken much interest in my work before then, but Ned found some of my ideas about labor markets intriguing and encouraged me to write a paper for a volume he was assembling.

Few people actually read edited volumes, so publishing a paper in an outlet like that isn't a particularly valuable career move for an academic economist. (The psychologist Danny

Kahneman, who won the Nobel Prize in economics in 2002, once told me that he urges young colleagues never to write a paper for an edited volume.) But since I was so far behind schedule, I readily agreed to Ned's proposal. I went right to work on the project and was pleased with the resulting paper.

Shortly after I'd given Ned my first draft of it, however, he came to my office with a crestfallen expression. He announced that the editor of the series in which the volume was to have appeared had just called to say that the project had been cancelled. Bad luck!

Or so it seemed. On a lark, I sent the paper to *Econometrica*, one of the most prestigious and selective journals in economics. Less than two months later, I received an acceptance letter from the editor with no demands for substantive revisions. Encouraged by that success, I dashed off a simple extension of the paper and submitted it to another leading journal. That editor's acceptance letter arrived only a few weeks later, again with no demand for significant changes.

The following summer, I wrote three more papers and sent them out for review. Bang, bang, bang, I quickly received acceptance letters from the editors of the *American Economic Review*, *Journal of Political Economy*, and the *Review of Economics and Statistics*, each a top-tier journal in economics that accepts less than 10 percent of papers submitted. And once more, there were no demands for substantive revisions.

In striking contrast, most of the scores of papers I've published since those early years were rejected by at least one journal, some by as many as four, and in only a few instances did I even receive an editorial decision before six months or more had elapsed. When my papers weren't rejected outright, editors invariably demanded extensive revisions, with no promise to publish before the changes had been carefully vetted, a step that extended the review process by at least several more months.

I remain proud of some of those first papers I submitted, but I firmly believe that the ones I've written in the years since are of generally higher quality. The only plausible conclusion is that my early run of editorial success occurred against astronomically long odds.

Had it not been for that exceptional good fortune, my senior colleagues almost surely would not have voted on my behalf when I came up for tenure at the beginning of my sixth year at Cornell. A friend who was in the meeting later told me that the committee in charge of my case had solicited reviews from distinguished outsiders who were known to be highly critical of almost everyone's work. The committee's clear hope, he said, was to assemble a dossier that would help it defend a negative decision in my case. In the end, however, my record on paper was significantly stronger than those of the others who'd been hired at the same time. To fire me, the department would have had to fire the others as well, a step that committee members apparently felt they couldn't defend.

So except for a wildly improbable string of chance events—if I hadn't been hired in the first place, if Ned Gramlich hadn't come as a visitor, if my papers had been rejected at what later proved to be my normal rate, or even if editors had just taken their usual sweet time to rule on them—I would never have enjoyed the opportunity to interact with so many intelligent and stimulating students and colleagues during the past decades. I wouldn't have been invited to so many interesting conferences. I wouldn't have received so many research grants. I wouldn't have been invited to spend ten days with the Dalai Lama in India, or to write an economics column for the *New York Times*. These and countless other rewarding experiences were mine to enjoy because I got lucky.

Is it possible to quantify the extent to which success in different domains depends on seemingly trivial chance events? The aforementioned sociologist Duncan Watts and his collaborators designed an experiment they called Music Lab in an attempt to answer this question for aspiring musicians. On a website, they posted the names of forty-eight indie bands and one song from each. My two youngest sons are the front men of The Nepotist, an indie band struggling to break out in the hyper-competitive New York City music scene, so I probably know more about indie bands than most people. But I had never heard of any of the bands posted on Music Lab.[9]

Visitors to the website could download any of the forty-eight songs on the condition that they provide a rating indicating how well they liked it. The researchers averaged the resulting responses to create an "objective" song quality rating—objective in the sense that these ratings were made without any knowledge by respondents of how other people were reacting to the songs. These objective ratings were highly variable. A handful of songs got high marks from most listeners, and a few got low marks from most. But for the substantial majority, there was no consistent response. Some people really liked these songs, others thought they were OK, and still others gave them extremely low ratings.

With those objective ratings in hand, the researchers then created eight independent websites that contained the same forty-eight bands and songs as before. But each of these new sites also displayed some additional information: Visitors could now see how many times each song had been downloaded and also the average quality rating it had received thus far.

One of the bands in the experiment was 52 Metro. Their song, "Lockdown," landed roughly in the middle of the objective scores, ranking 26th out of 48. This song's subsequent fate varied dramatically across the eight websites that incorporated social feedback. On one it ranked #1, but it was only #40 on another.

The song's fate, it turned out, depended largely on how the first people to download it happened to react to it. If they liked it a lot, that created a halo effect that made others more likely to download it and respond favorably. But if early downloaders happened not to like it, things went downhill.

The Music Lab findings suggest that many songs (or books or movies) that go on to become hits owe much of their success to the fact that the first people to review them just happened to like them. Works of unambiguously high quality are of course more likely to earn positive early reviews and may succeed even in the face of some negative early commentary. But most artistic endeavors elicit a broad range of subjective evaluations. Some go on to succeed simply because the first people to express their opinions about them publicly just happened to come from the right tail of the opinion distribution. Which is to say, many artistic endeavors owe their success, at least in part, to pure dumb luck.

Many successful artists seem blissfully unaware of that fact. But there are refreshing exceptions. Consider again Vince Gilligan, the creator of *Breaking Bad*. When Brett Martin interviewed him about the series' success for *GQ*'s Men of the Year issue in 2013, Gilligan had this to say:[10]

> Have you ever been sitting at your desk and you crumple up a piece of paper and, without even looking, you just toss it over your shoulder and it goes straight into the wastebasket? You didn't think about it. You didn't stress about it. You just did it. And now that you're thinking about it, you could never do it again in a million years, no matter how hard you tried. That's what this was like. We worked our butts off, but everybody works their butts off in TV. We tried to make the best show it was humanly possible to make, but you know, the guys on *According to*

Jim did the same thing. As to why this thing hit ... I could make up some stream of nonsense, but honestly ... I wish I could explain it, because then I might have a fighting chance on TV in the future. The truth is, I just have to be satisfied that it happened at all.

Small chance events often have big consequences. Identical twins take the SATs on the same Saturday. One of them is sick and scores 200 points lower than her sister, and their career trajectories start diverging from that day forward. One goes on to win a Nobel Prize in chemistry while the other struggles to get by as an adjunct chemistry lecturer. Even tiny variations often ramify into enormous differences in final outcomes.

Chance events also influence career trajectories by shaping people's decisions about what specialties to pursue. Childhood experience, which provides early clues about what sorts of things you're good at, may help you identify a market niche that seems to fit. But perhaps that niche is already filled, in which case you move on to the best remaining available one.

The birth order among siblings, which is as close to a pure chance result as any we can imagine, often plays a decisive role. My wife is the fifth of six children, five of them women. The athlete slot in her family was already taken when she came along, so she wasn't even considered for it. Instead, she got the artist/musician slot, which was a good fit for her talents and interests.

Even so, the athlete slot might have fit her even better. Having grown up in South Florida, I've taught several hundred people to water ski over the years. One of the first things novices do after learning to ski on two skis is to attempt the more difficult challenge of skiing on only one. Step one is to ski along on two skis, then kick one of them off while attempting to remain balanced on the remaining one. Once they've mastered that, they're ready to confront the really difficult part, which is to have the boat pull them out of the water on one ski. Among the hundreds of people I've tried to teach, my wife is the only one who succeeded on the very first attempt. It usually takes even the most gifted athletes many attempts.

My wife didn't even know that she was a good athlete until she was an adult, because the athlete's slot in her sibling cohort was already taken when she came along. And the fact that it was taken was just pure chance.

As the Williams sisters in tennis and the Alou brothers in baseball demonstrate, there can of course be more than one accomplished athlete in a sibling cohort. But the tendency I describe is real. My youngest son was for many years reluctant to embrace his passion for music because his older brother was such a standout in that domain. His passion won out, but it's easy to imagine that it might not have.

As Malcolm Gladwell explains at length in *Outliers*, early family advantage often explains individual differences in success.[11] Bill Gates, for example, had the good fortune as an eighth-grader in the late 1960s to attend one of the only private schools in the country that offered students unlimited access to one of the early time-share computer programming terminals. On those terminals, programmers for the first time were able to submit their programs and have them run immediately. Errors in syntax were flagged right away and could be corrected on the fly.

I'm ten years older than Gates, and instant feedback was not part of the package when I learned to program in college. In those days, we had to type our programs on punch cards, carry the decks up a long, steep hill, and then put them in a queue at the computer center. The next day, we'd climb that same hill to retrieve a printout that would list the various errors that had prevented our programs from running. We'd attempt corrections and resubmit our decks, and it was often several days before we had a program that would even run, much less do what we'd hoped.

Gates was born at a time and in circumstances that made him one of the first Americans able to spend long hours getting instant feedback for his programming efforts. When he was later asked how many other teens from his era had backgrounds similar to his before heading off to college, he said, "If there were 50 in the world, I'd be stunned. I had a better exposure to software development at a young age than I think anyone did in that period of time, and all because of an incredibly lucky series of events."[12]

Bill Gates would not have gone on to become one of the wealthiest people in the world if he had not achieved such deep mastery at writing software. But even coupled with his appetite for sustained hard work, that expertise does not fully explain his success. He was also fortunate in other important ways.

After dropping out of Harvard, he and his high school friend Paul Allen teamed up to form the company they would later call Microsoft. It was a propitious moment to launch a software development company, and their venture almost certainly would have prospered even in the absence of any lucky breaks. But Microsoft didn't just prosper. By the late 1990s, it had become the most valuable company on the planet.

A key step in its transition from a small tech start-up was when IBM approached Gates in 1980 to ask whether Microsoft could help create an operating system for the new personal computer it was developing. Gates was originally reluctant to take on the project and suggested that IBM contact Digital Research, another small Seattle software firm that had already developed a personal computer operating system called CP/M.

IBM spoke with Digital Research's founder, Gary Kildall, who expressed interest. Accounts differ as to how events unfolded after that meeting, but what's clear is that IBM and DR failed to reach an agreement on the sale of CP/M.[13] Jack Sams, the IBM negotiator in charge of procuring an operating system, later mentioned to Bill Gates that IBM was considering the possibility of acquiring QDOS, the so-called "quick and dirty operating system" written by Tim Patterson of Seattle Computer Products. Patterson had developed QDOS with Kildall's CP/M manual in hand and acknowledges that it was based closely on CP/M. But Patterson believed that QDOS was sufficiently different from CP/M to withstand legal challenge.

In the physicist and science writer Leonard Mlodinow's account of what happened next, "According to Sams, Gates said, 'Do you want to get ... [QDOS], or do you want me to?' Sams, apparently not appreciating the implications, said, 'By all means, you get it.'" With that statement, Sams unwittingly signed away an asset that would end up being worth hundreds of billions of dollars. Paul Allen negotiated Microsoft's purchase of QDOS for roughly $50,000. The company then modified the program further, and renamed it MS-DOS, for Microsoft disk operating system. IBM then agreed that Microsoft would receive a royalty payment for each of the new IBM PCs that used the operating system.

Gates's biggest stroke of luck sprang from IBM's pessimistic forecast of sales of its PCs. Had the company foreseen the explosive growth that loomed, it would never have permitted Microsoft to retain ownership of MS-DOS. But Microsoft got lucky, and the royalty fee it was able to charge for each installed copy of the operating system was the most important reason it became so spectacularly profitable.

In short, most of us would never have heard of Microsoft if any one of a long sequence of improbable events had not occurred. If Bill Gates had been born in 1945 rather than 1955, if his high school had not had a computer club with one of the first terminals that could offer instant feedback, if IBM had reached an agreement with Gary Kildall's Digital Research, or if Tim Paterson had been a more experienced negotiator, Gates almost certainly never would have succeeded on such a grand scale.

Sometimes, even seemingly unlucky starts turn out to make long-run success more likely. Gladwell cites the experience of Jews who immigrated to New York in the early twentieth century and went on to prosper in the garment industry. Many raised children who graduated from law school, only to be rejected by leading New York law firms, which in those days hired mostly lawyers from wealthy Protestant families. Jewish graduates were often left with few better options than to start small firms of their own. Those firms often specialized in cases that the elite law firms felt were beneath them, such as the litigation of hostile corporate takeovers. The lawyers raised by garment workers were thus often the only ones who had developed the expertise to capitalize on the explosive growth of hostile takeover litigation that occurred in the 1970s and 1980s. By dominating that new market, they went on to earn vastly more than the lawyers in the firms that had earlier shunned them.

My own family background made me lucky in a somewhat different way. The adopted son of two Florida chiropractors, I grew up with an X-ray machine in my living room, and although I never went to bed hungry, money was usually tight. I knew that if there was something special I wanted, I needed to earn it on my own—at first by shining shoes in bars, later by delivering newspapers before dawn. It wasn't until I was in my midthirties that I met my birth mother and her extended family and learned how different my surroundings would have been if I hadn't been given up for adoption. They welcomed me graciously, and in due course I discovered that they were a Cape Cod family of long distinction. A large oil portrait of Frederic Tudor, one of my great-great grandfathers, hangs in the Baker Library at Harvard.

The Ice King: Frederic Tudor, 1783–1864.

Tudor was known as the Ice King. In the nineteenth century, he became one of New England's richest men by stubbornly pursuing an idea that most others ridiculed: harvesting ice in winter from New England ponds and transporting it by ship to hot-weather cities around the globe. Gavin Weightman's biography of him is a case study of resilience in the face of adversity.[14] Tudor went bankrupt several times and served several sentences in debtors' prisons, but he prevailed in the end. A dwindling share of his once massive fortune has been passed on through the generations ever since.

Most of my cousins thus grew up knowing that significant trust funds awaited them upon reaching adulthood. That knowledge wouldn't affect everybody in the same way—Bill Gates came from a well-to-do family, and no one ever questioned his willingness to work hard—but I know how it would have affected me. How do you summon the will to do the difficult things you must do to get a career on track if you know that a lot of money is coming your way soon in any event? I just don't think I would have enjoyed a career nearly as interesting as the one I've had if I'd grown up with a lot of money.

Countless other examples attest to the power of seemingly minor random factors to alter life trajectories in major ways. In hockey, for instance, roughly 40 percent of all players in the premier professional leagues around the world were born in January, February, or March, while only 10 percent were born in October, November, or December.[15] The apparent reason for this skewed distribution is that January 1 is the traditional cut-off birth date for participation in youth hockey leagues. Players born early in the year were thus the oldest members of their team at each successive stage. On average, they were slightly bigger, stronger, faster, and more experienced than their teammates born in later months. Because they were more likely to excel at each stage, they were more likely to be chosen for elite traveling teams and for all-star teams. They were more likely to be funneled into the programs with the best facilities and the best coaching, more likely to receive athletic scholarships, and so on.[16]

Similar links between birth dates and achievement show up in other domains. Although school start dates vary from place to place, most children born in the summer months tend to be among the youngest members of their class. That simple fact appears to explain why those students are significantly less likely to hold leadership positions during their high school years.[17] Other studies have found that even after controlling for cognitive ability and other psychological and physical traits, students who hold leadership positions go on to earn significantly higher wages.[18] And researchers who studied a sample of large American companies found that the number of CEOs born in June and July is almost one-third lower than would be expected on the basis of chance.[19]

Even the first letter of a person's last name can help to explain significant achievement differences. One study, for example, found that assistant professors in the ten top-ranked economics departments were more likely to be promoted to tenure the earlier the first letter of their last name fell in the alphabet. The study's authors attributed this effect to the custom in economics of listing authors' names alphabetically on coauthored papers, noting that they found no similar effect for professors in psychology, which does not list authors alphabetically.[20]

To acknowledge that seemingly trivial random events often matter enormously is not to suggest that success in life is independent of talent and effort. In the most competitive arenas, those who do well are almost invariably both highly talented and incredibly hardworking. As Charlie Munger, the vice-chairman of Warren Buffett's Berkshire Hathaway, has written, "The safest way to try to get what you want is to try to deserve what you want." Perhaps the most useful advice for someone who aspires to material success is to develop deep expertise at a task that others value highly. And expertise comes not from luck but from thousands of hours of difficult effort.

Yet chance events also matter. And as we'll see, material success in many arenas is almost impossible without a substantial measure of good luck.

3
♠

HOW WINNER-TAKE-ALL
MARKETS MAGNIFY LUCK'S ROLE

Why do hardworking people with similar talents and training often earn such dramatically different incomes? And why, too, have these earnings gaps grown so much larger in recent decades? Almost no other questions have proved more enduringly fascinating to economists.

The traditional approach to these questions views labor markets as perfectly competitive meritocracies in which people are paid in accordance with the value of what they produce. In this view, earnings differences result largely from individual differences in "human capital"—an amalgam of intelligence, training, experience, social skills, and other personal characteristics known to affect productivity. Human capital commands a rate of return in the marketplace, just like any other asset, suggesting that individual pay differences should be proportional to the corresponding differences in human capital. So, for example, if Sue has twice as much human capital as James, her earnings should be roughly twice as large.

But not even the most sophisticated measures of human capital can explain more than a tiny fraction of individual earnings differences during any year. And since the distributions of intelligence, experience, and other traits across individuals don't seem to have changed much during the past few decades, the human capital approach has little to say about growing pay disparities over time.

The human capital approach is also completely silent about the role of chance events in the labor market. It assumes that the more human capital you have, the more you get paid, which obviously isn't always the case. Of course, most people in the top 1 percent didn't get there *just* by being lucky. Almost all of them work extremely hard and are unusually good at what they do. They have *lots* of human capital. But what the human capital approach misses is that certain skills are far more valuable in some settings than in others. In our 1995 book, *The Winner-Take-All Society*, Philip Cook and I argued that a gifted salesperson, for example, will be far more productive if her assignment is to sell financial securities to sovereign wealth funds than if she's selling children's shoes.[1]

If markets have been growing more competitive over time, why are the earnings gaps unaccounted for by the human capital approach larger than ever? Cook and I argued that what's been changing is that new technologies and market institutions have been providing growing leverage for the talents of the ablest individuals. The best option available to patients suffering from a rare illness was once to consult with the most knowledgeable local practitioner. But now that medical records can be sent anywhere with a single mouse click, today's patients can receive advice from the world's leading authority on that illness.

Such changes didn't begin yesterday. Alfred Marshall, the great nineteenth-century British economist, described how advances in transportation enabled the best producers in almost every domain to extend their reach. Piano manufacturing, for instance, was once widely dispersed, simply because pianos were so costly to transport. Unless they were produced close to where buyers lived, shipping costs quickly became prohibitive.

But with each extension of the highway, rail, and canal systems, shipping costs fell sharply, and at each step production became more concentrated. Worldwide, only a handful of the best piano producers now survive. It's of course a good thing that their superior offerings are now available to more people. But an inevitable side effect has been that producers with even a slight edge over their rivals went on to capture most of the industry's income.

Therein lies a hint about why chance events have grown more important even as markets have become more competitive. When shipping costs fell dramatically, producers who were once local monopolists serving geographically isolated markets found themselves battling one another for survival. In those battles, even a tiny cost advantage or quality edge could be decisive. Minor random events can easily tip the balance in such competitions—and in the process spell the difference between great wealth and economic failure. So luck is becoming more important in part because the stakes have increased sharply in contests whose outcomes have always hinged partly on chance events.

Many of the environmental changes that have been occurring over time are analogous to reductions in shipping costs. That's true, for example, of reductions in tariff barriers and better communication technologies. Perhaps even more important has been the fact that an increasing share of what makes a product valuable is accounted for by the ideas embedded in it. Ideas don't weigh anything so are costless to ship.

Cook and I argued that these changes help explain both the growing income differences between ostensibly similar individuals and the surge in income inequality that began in the late 1960s. In domain after domain, we wrote, technology has been enabling the most gifted performers to extend their reach.

Local accountants were displaced in two waves—first by franchised services like H&R Block and more recently by tax software for the masses. Brick-and-mortar shops have been going out of business at a rapid clip, replaced by Amazon and other online retailers. And whereas the best tire producer in, say, Akron, Ohio, was once assured of a vibrant local market, drivers now buy from only a handful of the best producers worldwide.

Reasons for such displacements differ from case to case. But an important contributing factor in almost all cases has been the information revolution. In the 1950s, telephone connections across the Atlantic were so scarce that some international firms hired clerks in the United States to spend their entire workday reading texts over the phone to their counterparts in European branches, just to keep the lines open. In those days, international corporate operations were heavily constrained by the practical difficulties of coordination and control. For a firm to survive in that era, it was often enough to be the best producer in a fairly narrow locale.

But both the scale and scope of individual markets have grown enormously in the intervening years. When one seller's offering is better than all others, word quickly spreads. Lower shipping costs, coupled with falling trade barriers, have made it easier than ever to serve buyers everywhere. The upshot is that if an economic opportunity arises anywhere in the networked world, ambitious entrepreneurs are quickly able to discover and exploit it.

Modern communications technology has also reinforced powerful network effects that have increased the rewards to top performers. Those effects helped explain the growing dominance of the Windows PC platform during the late 1980s. Once

Microsoft's Windows graphical user interface reached parity with earlier rival Apple's Macintosh, the numerical superiority of Windows users became a decisive advantage. Software developers concentrated their efforts on the Windows platform because more users meant more sales. And the greater availability of software titles, in turn, lured still more users to Windows, creating a positive feedback loop in the form of a network effect that drove Apple to the brink of bankruptcy.

Network effects sometimes permit one firm's ephemeral advantage to defeat a rival's otherwise superior offering, as apparently happened in the battle between Betamax and VHS several decades ago. In the late 1980s, I purchased my first video cassette recorder, one of the last in my circle of friends to do so. I vividly recall the salesman's conclusive demonstration of the superiority of Sony's Betamax format over the competing VHS format from JVC. Although I agreed with him that the Betamax picture was much sharper, he didn't seem the least bit surprised when I announced my decision to buy the VHS machine instead.

The problem for Betamax was that early versions permitted users to record at most only 60 minutes of content at a time. And since one of the main reasons for owning a VCR was to record televised movies, that was a serious drawback. When VHS offered customers the chance to record for two hours at a time, sales quickly began tipping in its favor, despite its inferior picture quality.

Once the installed base of VHS machines exceeded that of Betamax, Blockbuster and other video rental shops began tilting their rental stocks in favor of VHS titles, which in turn further increased the attractiveness of that format.

Another popular use of VCRs at the time was for people to send home videos to their children's grandparents. But that worked only if both households used the same format, so here was an additional positive feedback loop that reinforced the reasons for choosing VHS. In the meantime, Sony had managed to extend Betamax recording times. But by then the downward spiral was well underway, and Betamax was doomed.

Network effects merit special emphasis because they are perhaps the most important source of randomness in high-stakes winner-take-all contests. One reason for reading a book or seeing a film is to enjoy the experience of discussing it with others. Opportunities for such exchanges are of course more numerous when you read best-selling titles or watch popular films. But of the thousands of entries released in any given year, only a relative handful find their way onto the most widely circulated best-seller lists.

Whether a book becomes a best seller depends on many factors, perhaps the most important of which is whether it's any good. But as their authors can attest, many good books never achieve best-seller status. It is far more likely that a book of given quality will become a best seller if it was written by an author of earlier best sellers. Among first-time best sellers, most are books that enjoyed strongly favorable reviews in prominent outlets like the *New York Times* or the *Atlantic*. But most books, like most other artistic endeavors, elicit a spectrum of reactions from reviewers. As illustrated by the Music Lab experiments discussed earlier, a disproportionate number of best sellers will thus have been written by fortunate authors whose books were assigned to initial reviewers who happened to like them. Many best sellers are no more worthy, in purely objective terms, than a host of other books that fail to make the list.

Winner-take-all markets generally display two characteristic features. One is that rewards depend less on absolute performance than on relative performance. Steffi Graf, one of the best female tennis players of all time, played at a consistently high level throughout the mid-1990s, yet she earned considerably more during the twelve months after April 1993 than during the preceding twelve months. One reason was the absence during the latter period of her rival Monica Seles, who had been forced to leave the tour after being stabbed in the back that April by a deranged fan at a tournament in Germany. Although the absolute quality of Graf's play didn't change much during Seles's absence, her relative quality improved substantially.

A second important feature of winner-take-all markets is that rewards tend to be highly concentrated in the hands of a few top performers. That can occur for many reasons, but most often it's a consequence of production technologies that extend a given performer's reach. That's true, for example, in the music industry, which exhibits both features of winner-take-all markets. As the economist Sherwin Rosen wrote,

> The market for classical music has never been larger than it is now, yet the number of full-time soloists on any given instrument is on the order of only a few hundred (and much smaller for instruments other than voice, violin, and piano). Performers of the first rank comprise a limited handful out of these small totals and have very large incomes. There are also known to be substantial differences between [their incomes and the incomes of] those in the second rank, even though most consumers would have difficulty detecting more than minor differences in a "blind" hearing.[2]

One hundred years ago, the only way to listen to music was to attend a live performance. Then as now, opera buffs wanted to hear the most renowned singers perform, but there were only so many live events those musicians could stage during any given year. And so there was a robust market for thousands of sopranos and tenors on the worldwide tour. The lesser-ranked performers earned less than their higher-ranked colleagues, but not that much less. Now, lifelike recording technologies enable fans to hear their favorite operas reproduced faithfully at home. And those who demand the entire stage spectacle can now watch HD broadcasts of performances of the New York Metropolitan Opera Company in theaters around the globe. All the while, local opera companies have been closing their doors.

Once critics and audiences reach consensus on who the best performers are, the market for recorded or televised operas can be served by only a small handful of artists. Most people today would have difficulty naming more than three tenors. That's because the market no longer "needs" more than a handful of tenors. Once the master recording of a tenor's performance has been made, it's essentially costless to make additional copies of it. That's also why a small handful of artists land seven-figure recording contracts, even as thousands of others—many of them nearly as talented—struggle to get by as elementary school music teachers.

Some of the same technological forces that have tended to concentrate rewards also exert countervailing effects. As Chris Anderson explained in his 2006 book *The Long Tail*, digital technology has been making music, books, movies, and many other goods economically viable on a much smaller scale than ever before.[3]

In past decades, for example, a film could generate revenue only by mustering audiences of sufficient size to justify screenings in movie theaters. Most niche markets—think Hindi-language movies in medium-size American cities—were simply not viable. That changed with Netflix. Since the marginal cost of shipping a digital movie is essentially zero, it's now possible for people to watch it without having to assemble a theater full of ticket buyers. In principle, at least, this creates exciting new possibilities for small-scale sellers.

Anderson's long-tail account and the winner-take-all account both capture important aspects of how technology has been altering people's options. But preliminary evidence suggests that the winner-take-all account has tracked the observed trends more closely.

Consider digital music sales. Long-tail proponents predict that market shares of the most popular songs should be decreasing in favor of the weakest selling titles. But as the Harvard Business School professor Anita Elberse recounts in her carefully researched 2013 book, the numbers suggest otherwise.[4] The top one-thousandth of 1 percent of song titles now account for a much larger proportion of sales (15 percent in 2011, up from only 7 percent in 2007).

Trends for weak-selling titles have also been running counter to the long-tail prediction. The proportion of titles selling fewer than one hundred copies annually, for example, was 94 percent in 2011, up from 91 percent in 2007. (This was a period during which overall sales nearly doubled, so sales of these slow-moving titles were growing substantially in absolute terms.)

The market shares of top offerings have also been growing in the publishing and film industries, according to Elberse. In some cases, they've been gaining ground because social media have amplified their attractiveness. Here again, we see the influence of network effects. Simple arithmetic ensures that Facebook exchanges are far more likely to be stimulated by posts on best-selling titles.

Another factor is that new technology has done little to relieve an important market constraint—the scarcity of people's time and energy. No one could possibly examine each of the million-plus offerings in Apple's app store. And as the Swarthmore psychologist Barry Schwartz argued in his 2004 book, *The Paradox of Choice*, most people find it unpleasant to sift through a plethora of options.[5] Many people sidestep that problem by focusing on only the most popular entries in each category.

But the mere fact that top sellers are becoming even more popular doesn't mean that the long tail's promise of a golden age of small-scale creative energy has been empty. It has indeed become less costly for producers to target buyers with highly idiosyncratic tastes, and sophisticated search algorithms increasingly enable such buyers to find just the quirky offerings they're looking for.

Creative people have never faced better opportunities to display their talent. Websites and YouTube links place their songs and stories within easy reach of almost everyone. These channels have become the new minor leagues for producing tomorrow's superstars. And because the cost of access is so low, markets for creative endeavor are becoming far more meritocratic than their earlier counterparts.

These issues strike close to home. I placed my intellectual bets long ago on the winner-take-all perspective. Yet I also have a strong personal rooting interest in Anderson's long-tail perspective. Earlier I mentioned The Nepotist, the alternative-soul band fronted by my two youngest sons, Chris and Hayden. They're still a long way from being able to make ends meet without the help of their day jobs. But they've been steadily climbing the ladder. Perhaps I'm biased in believing they're good enough to make it.[6] If they do break out, spectacular rewards could follow. But they're well aware that their odds of stardom remain almost vanishingly small.

The forces driving recent trends in CEO pay shed additional light on how small differences in performance can translate into enormous differences in earnings. Consider a company with $10 billion in annual earnings that has narrowed its CEO search to two finalists, one slightly more talented than the other—by enough, say, to cause a 3 percent swing in the company's bottom line. Even that minuscule talent difference would translate into an additional $300 million in earnings. Even if the better performer were paid $100 million, that person would still be a bargain.

CEO leverage has been growing quickly as firms have expanded in size. As the New York University economists Xavier Gabaix and Augustin Landier argued in a 2008 paper, executive pay in a competitive market should vary in direct proportion to the market capitalization of the company.[7] They found that CEO compensation at large companies grew sixfold between 1980 and 2003, roughly the same as the market-cap growth of these businesses.

But growth in executive leverage alone cannot explain the explosive increase in executive salaries. The decisions made by Charles Erwin Wilson, who headed General Motors from 1941 to 1953, had as big an impact on that company's annual bottom line as the corresponding decisions by today's average Fortune 500 CEO. Yet Wilson's total career earnings at GM, after adjusting for inflation, were just a fraction of what today's top CEOs earn every year.

That's because a second factor necessary to explain explosive CEO pay growth—an open market for CEOs—didn't exist in Wilson's day. Until recently, most corporate boards shared an implicit belief that the only credible candidates for top executive positions were employees who had spent all or most of their careers with the company. There was usually a leading internal candidate to succeed a retiring CEO, and seldom more than a few others who were even credible. Under the circumstances, CEO pay was a matter of bilateral negotiation between the board and the anointed successor.

That focus on insiders has softened in recent decades, a change driven in no small part by one particularly visible outside hire. That would be Louis J. Gerstner, who was hired away from RJR Nabisco by IBM in 1993. At the time, outside observers were extremely skeptical that a former tobacco CEO would be able to turn the struggling computer giant around. But IBM's board felt that Gerstner's motivational and managerial talents were just what the company needed and that subordinates could compensate for any technical gaps in Gerstner's knowledge. The company's bet paid off spectacularly, of course, and in the ensuing years the trend toward outside CEO hires has accelerated across most industries.

Most companies still promote CEOs from within, but even in those cases, the more open market for executive talent has completely transformed the climate in which salary negotiations take place. Internal candidates can now threaten credibly to move if they're not paid in accordance with the market's estimate of their economic value.

The more open market conditions have affected executive salaries in much the same way that free agency affected the salaries of professional athletes. CEOs of the largest American corporations, who were paid forty-two times as much as the average worker as recently as 1980, are now paid more than four hundred times as much. So once more we see the growing importance of the seemingly minor random events that produce small differences in absolute performance.

Greater competition also creates positive feedback effects that amplify the growth of salaries at the top of a variety of industries by altering spending patterns. Such effects appear to help explain growing inequality among dentists, for example. The dentists whose earnings have grown the most dramatically are often specialists in cosmetic dentistry, the demand for whose services has been fueled by higher top salaries in other occupations. And the highest paid dentists, in turn, often demand the services of the most highly paid specialists in other fields.

Recent trends in the distributions of income represent a substantial departure from those observed during the first three decades after WWII, when pretax incomes in America grew at roughly the same rate—slightly less than 3 percent a year—for households up and down the income ladder. Since the late 1960s, this pattern has changed. The inflation-adjusted median hourly wage for American men is actually lower now than it was then. Real median household incomes grew by roughly 19 percent between 1967 and 2012, primarily because of large increases in female labor force participation. Only those in the top quintile, whose incomes have roughly doubled since the mid-1970s, have escaped the income slowdown. Similar, if less dramatic, changes have been observed in most other countries.

The income growth picture is much the same within each subgroup of the population as for the population as a whole. For example, those at the bottom of the top quintile have seen little real income growth, the lion's share of which has been concentrated among top earners in the group. Real incomes among the top 5 percent, for example, were more than two and a half times larger in 2007 than in 1979, while those among the top 1 percent were almost four times larger. In 1976, only 8.9 percent of the nation's total pretax incomes went to the top 1 percent of earners, but by 2012 that group was receiving 22.5 percent of the total.

The winner-take-all account of rising inequality has not persuaded everyone. Some critics complain, for example, that the explosive growth of CEO pay proves that executive labor markets are not really competitive—that CEOs appoint cronies to their boards who approve unjustifiably large pay packages. We're also told that industrial behemoths conspire to drive out their rivals, thereby extorting higher prices from captive customers.

To be sure, such abuses occur. But they're no worse now than they've always been. As Adam Smith wrote in *The Wealth of*

Nations, "People of the same trade seldom meet together, even for merriment and diversion, but the conversation ends in a conspiracy against the public, or in some contrivance to raise prices."[8] CEOs have always appointed people they know to their boards, so that's not enough to explain recent trends.

Critics are also quick to point out that unsuccessful CEOs receive the same huge compensation packages as their more successful counterparts. That's true in any given year, but the relationship between pay and performance emerges more clearly once we examine a longer time horizon. In every labor market, there tends to be a going rate for those who perform the most important tasks, whether they be executives in business or coaches in professional sports. The more important the leadership position is, the higher the going rate. In most domains, it's extremely difficult to predict which candidates will perform best. Hiring committees generally appoint the ones they think best, and compensate them at rates in accord with what excellent performance would justify.

But companies are quicker than ever to cut their losses when performance disappoints. Relative to earlier decades, today's executives are on a much tighter leash, and those who fail to deliver are quickly sent packing. Léo Apotheker, for example, was named CEO of Hewlett-Packard in November 2010 only to be discharged in September 2011 after the company's share prices had plunged sharply under his leadership. CEOs of S&P 500 companies who left their posts in 2012 had 20 percent shorter tenures, on average, than their counterparts from 2000.[9]

Some attribute rising inequality to growth in the "skill premium," the higher wage that employers must offer in order to attract the increasing number of highly skilled workers they need. Yes, the earnings differential between college graduates and others is now wider than it was thirty years ago. Yet if we look only at the distribution of earnings among college graduates, we see the same pattern as for society as a whole. For most college graduates, wage increases have been either small or nonexistent in recent decades. The premium for college graduates exists because a relatively small number of the most successful graduates have enjoyed spectacular earnings growth during the same period.

Others argue that globalization has boosted inequality by forcing down the wages of the least skilled workers. Here, too, there's a measure of truth. Unions, for example, have lost some of their bargaining power as firms have become better able to move their operations to low-wage countries. Outsourcing via the Internet has put similar downward pressure on wages.

But these global pressures do not account for what's been happening in the white-collar professions. The growing inequality at the top is even more dramatic than at the bottom, as the most highly compensated corporate managers, lawyers, physicians, and even preachers have pulled away from the pack. In short, growth in inequality does not appear to have resulted from growing market imperfections or from increased outsourcing to lower-paid workers in developing countries.

Events of the past two decades have provided little reason to doubt that runaway growth in top incomes has resulted in large part from increasing leverage in the "winners" positions, in tandem with growing competition to fill those positions. By every measure, markets have grown more competitive, and the most productive players have gained additional leverage since *The Winner-Take-All Society*'s publication in 1995.

What's also clear is that the economic forces that have been causing the spread and intensification of winner-take-all markets have by no means run their course. We can expect continued growth in the intensity of competition on the buyers' side for the best talent, and on the sellers' side for the top positions.

In his widely discussed 2013 book, *Capital in the Twenty-First Century*, Thomas Piketty suggested yet another reason for rising inequality, which is the historical tendency for the rate of return on invested capital to exceed the overall growth rate for the economy.[10] When that happens, he argues, wealth continues to concentrate in the hands of those who own the most capital. All things considered, then, it appears prudent to envision a future characterized by continued growth in income and wealth inequality—which is to say, a future in which chance events will become still more important.

Because the enormous prizes at stake in many arenas attract so many contestants, the winners will almost without exception be enormously talented and hardworking. But as we'll see in the next chapter, they will rarely be the *most* talented and hardworking people in the contestant pool. We'll see, too, that even in contests in which luck plays only a minuscule role, winners will almost always be among the luckiest of all contestants.

The upshot is that with far greater frequency than ever before, seemingly trivial chance events give rise to spectacular differences in economic reward.

4
♠

WHY THE BIGGEST WINNERS
ARE ALMOST ALWAYS LUCKY

Reddit, the online forum, once asked its readers, "What's the most statistically improbable thing that ever happened to you?" The question provoked some interesting responses.

One person wrote, for example, "In the middle of making an omelette, I answered the door while holding a whole egg. It turned out to be my new neighbor asking if she could borrow an egg. The look of confusion on her face when I produced one on the spot was matched only by my own. She took it and left without saying a word."

I've never answered my door with an egg in hand. Nor has a neighbor ever knocked on my door asking to borrow one. So at my age I feel reasonably confident that I'll never have an experience precisely like the one described.

Over the years, however, neighbors have occasionally knocked to ask whether they could borrow something, usually a cooking ingredient or utensil. Most of those requests came at mealtimes, and it would not have seemed at all strange for a neighbor to have requested an egg. And since I often cook with eggs, it's also easy to imagine answering the door with an egg in hand. So I can easily imagine both events having happened to me. But the odds of both occurring at the same time are truly remote. That's why almost none of us will ever experience the specific chain of events described.

But for us collectively, the odds of that chain of events happening aren't minuscule at all. In the United States alone there are hundreds of millions of adults and therefore hundreds of millions of breakfast hours each day. Let twenty years pass and we have more than a trillion breakfast hours during which the events described could have occurred to *someone*. It seems safe to say that many more than one—and since we're talking about eggs here, perhaps even dozens—of such experiences must have already occurred in this country alone.

The huge difference between the likelihood of a strange event happening to you now and the likelihood of that event happening to someone, sometime, clouds our intuition about highly improbable events. In any one person's life, nothing unusual happens most of the time. Yet virtually everyone who lives long enough will witness a few events that seem to defy belief. Most of these events are merely highly unlikely to happen in any given moment. But the more moments you string together, the more likely they become. And if you string together enough moments across enough people, events that are prohibitively unlikely in any given instance suddenly become all but inevitable.

The strangest coincidence I have ever experienced personally arose in connection with my search for my birth mother. I don't remember ever not knowing that I was adopted, so my adoptive parents must have told me about it at a very early age. They also told me that they knew the names, birthplaces, and a few other facts about my birth parents and were prepared to share that information with me at any time.

I passed on that offer for several decades. It's not that I wasn't curious. I felt *very* different from my adoptive parents and was in fact quite interested to learn more about my origins. Yet I wasn't eager to deal with any of the disappointments that finding out about my birth parents might entail.

By age thirty-five, however, I felt settled enough to confront even the worst outcome I could imagine, which was to be rejected by parents who also happened to be thoroughly nasty people. So in 1980, I asked my adoptive mother to give me whatever information she had.

Thus I learned that my birth mother's maiden name had been Jane Garland, that she'd grown up on Cape Cod, had gone to Smith College, and had been a pilot ferrying planes between army bases in Florida during the war. She'd gotten pregnant by a naval officer stationed there. Marriage wasn't an option, not least because he was already engaged to a woman in the city where he'd grown up. So Jane decided to put me up for adoption. She somehow happened to know my adoptive father socially, who told her that he knew of a couple who were desperately seeking a child. He offered to help arrange the details of the adoption, without mentioning that he and his wife would be the adopting couple.

The first step in my search was to call Smith College to ask whether they could give me contact information for an alumna by the name of Jane Garland. They confirmed that a woman of that name had, in fact, attended Smith in the early 1940s but had dropped out after a year. They couldn't provide contact information, but they were able to tell me that her hometown had been Buzzards Bay, Massachusetts.

I then called directory assistance in Buzzards Bay and asked whether they had a listing for Jane Garland. No, but they did have four other Garlands—Christopher, David, Tudor, and one other. I took all four numbers and decided to call Tudor first. When a woman answered, I said I'd like to speak with Jane Garland but wasn't sure whether I had the right number. "Oh, you mean Jane Kramer," she said. "She's now living in Virginia." When I asked for Jane's number, she said she didn't have it but could give me the number of Jane's daughter Dana. That was the first I knew that I had a sister. (More than three decades later, I discovered that I have another!)

Because I didn't know whether Dana even knew about me, I was reluctant to call her directly. A historian friend at Cornell who'd been helping me with my search for Jane offered to call Dana and say that she was doing a study on women who'd gone to women's colleges in the 1940s and that Jane had ended up in her random sample. I didn't like the idea of deceiving Dana, but it seemed kinder than springing this news on her without talking to our mother first, so I agreed. My friend called Dana, who was happy to provide Jane's contact information. Now I had both Jane's phone number and her address in Delaplane, Virginia, a town so small that I couldn't find it on any of the maps I had.

At that point, I wasn't sure how to proceed. I didn't know whether Jane had a husband, and if so whether he knew about me, so I worried that a letter or call from me could cause her enormous difficulty. I considered driving down to Delaplane and doing a little digging around on my own in an effort to learn something about her situation. After pondering that possibility for a few days, I had by far the strangest experience of my life, before or since.

At the time, I was living across the street from a woman named Susan Miller, who I knew had grown up somewhere in Virginia. When I ran into her one afternoon, I asked whether she knew where Delaplane was. She blanched and asked why I wanted to know. She knew I'd been searching for my mother, and when I told her that I'd managed to find her address in Delaplane, she said, "I grew up in Delaplane! What's her name??"

When I told her, she shouted, "I know Jane Kramer!" She also knew Dana very well because they'd sat right next to each other during the first eight grades at the Hill Country Day School near Delaplane, where seats were assigned alphabetically. Susan told me that Jane had been married briefly to Dana's father, a man named Mooney, and then to someone named Kramer, but that she'd been living alone for at least the past twenty years.

Armed with that knowledge, I felt free to write Jane a letter. I vividly recall that my main concern while drafting it was to reassure her that I didn't need anything. I had a good job, was in sound financial health, didn't need any organ transplants, and so on. My only wish, I said, was to meet her and learn more about her. When I slipped that letter into the mailbox, I recall feeling *really* nervous about what sorts of turmoil it might unleash.

A few days later, I came home to find a message that Jane had called. I dialed her number and when she picked up I introduced myself. She immediately acknowledged that she was indeed my mother and was glad that I'd managed to find her, saying that she'd always wondered what had become of me.

She told me that her daughter had not in fact known about me, adding that Dana had always wanted a brother and had recruited several neighbor boys to act in that capacity while she was growing up. She told me that after getting my letter she'd called Dana, who was thrilled with the news. We chatted for a while longer, and before hanging up I said I would call Dana next and hoped that we could all find an opportunity to meet sometime soon.

When I reached Dana, she said she wanted to come to meet me right away. At the time she was working as a flight instructor at a small airport near her house in Buzzards Bay, and she asked whether it would be OK if she flew to Ithaca the next day if she could get a plane. Of course! She called back to say that she'd arranged everything and would be arriving at the Ithaca airport around 11:00 the next morning. I was there waiting when I saw her plane approach in a crystal blue June sky. She landed gracefully and climbed down out of the cockpit with a broad smile on her face.

What a thrill to meet her! My first two sons, who were twelve and ten then, were the first two blood relatives I'd ever known, but now I had a third! She parked her plane, and I drove us downtown to a waterfront restaurant for lunch.

When I noticed she wasn't eating much, I asked whether she normally didn't have much appetite. She said no, that she was usually a good eater but was just too excited to eat that day. She then mentioned in passing that she'd clipped a *New Yorker* cartoon years earlier that showed a Chinese mother admonishing her toddler for not eating: "Eat your rice, Han Ling, don't you know there are children in West Virginia who are starving?"

Most people wouldn't be much amused by that cartoon today. But when people our age were growing up, parents rarely missed an opportunity to say, "Eat your food, don't you know there are children in China who are starving?" What astonished me was that I had clipped *that very same cartoon* and pinned it to the bulletin board in my college dorm room more than fifteen years earlier! And it was one that I too mentioned occasionally when sharing meals with picky eaters.

Tastes in art and humor are highly idiosyncratic and may also have a heritable component. So perhaps there was some shared strand of DNA that caused each of us to react so strongly to that cartoon. But I can't think of any similar explanation for how Dana's childhood classmate came to be living across the street from me decades later. The odds that someone from Delaplane,

Virginia, a town that almost no one has ever heard of, would be my neighbor in Ithaca, another town that most people haven't heard of, are surely lower than those of getting heads twenty times in a row when flipping a fair coin. Many friends who have heard this story insist that the connection must have been more than just a coincidence—that it must have been fate, or the result of some sort of divine intervention.

But the real message, I believe, is far simpler: if you live long enough, you're bound to experience something profoundly improbable. The probability of getting heads 20 times in a row when flipping a fair coin is about 0.000001, meaning roughly that you'd expect to see it happen once every million times you tried. Most of the things we experience in life are the result of complex combinations of events, so a normal lifespan containing many millions of events is bound to include a few that seem stupefyingly improbable.

And so it is with the contests that determine who gets society's biggest economic prizes.

With tens of millions of other American boys, I once shared the dream of becoming a professional baseball player. But the process of making that dream a reality requires clearing a succession of increasingly difficult hurdles. By the time players reach high school, most will have abandoned their quest, voluntarily or involuntarily. But even at that point, a large absolute number of others remain in the hunt.

According to the High School Baseball Web, there are more than 450,000 players on the almost 15,000 teams listed by the National Federation of High Schools.[1] Of the more than 140,000 players eligible for the professional baseball draft each year, only 1,500 are selected. And since each of the 30 Major League Baseball teams can carry only 25 players on its roster, most of those 1,500 will never play a single inning of Major League Baseball.

Of course, the biggest winners in this particular contest are rewarded very handsomely indeed. In 2014, Miguel Cabrera, the first baseman for the Detroit Tigers, signed an eight-year contract extension for $248 million, an average of $31 million a year. Little wonder so many choose to enter the growing number of contests with similarly high stakes.

Chance events are more likely to be decisive in any competition as the number of contestants increases. That's because winning a competition with a large number of contestants requires that almost everything go right. And that, in turn, means that even when luck counts for only a trivial part of overall performance, there's rarely a winner who wasn't also very lucky.

Luck's role in such contests is closely analogous to the influence of wind in certain track and field events. To set a world record in track and field is an athletic achievement of the highest order. Without exception, the athletes who set them were born with almost superhuman levels of talent and the willingness to endure years of rigorous training. But even here the vagaries of chance play a pivotal role. To set a record, virtually everything must go right.

In four events—the 100-meter dash, the 110-meter hurdles (100 meters for women), the long jump, and the triple jump—performances are affected in small but measurable ways by the presence of headwinds or tailwinds. For that reason, the sport's governing bodies have ruled that performances are ineligible for world record status if they took place with a tailwind of more than 2 meters per second.

In table 4.1, note that of the eight current world records listed, seven occurred in the presence of a tailwind, none with a headwind. Seven of the eight previous holders of those records had also benefited from tailwinds (the lone exception being the men's 100 meters, which had neither headwind nor tailwind).[2]

TABLE 4.1. THE INFLUENCE OF WIND IN WORLD RECORD-SETTING TRACK AND FIELD PERFORMANCES

Men's Event	World Record	Athlete	Date	Wind
100 m	9.58 sec	Usain Bolt	16 Aug 2009	0.9 m/sec tailwind
110 m hurdles	12.80 sec	Aries Merritt	7 Sept 2012	0.3 m/sec tailwind
Long jump	8.93 m	Mike Powell	30 Aug 1991	0.3 m/sec tailwind
Triple jump	18.29 m	Jonathan Edwards	7 Aug 1995	1.3 m/sec tailwind
Women's Event	World Record	Athlete	Date	Wind
100 m	10.49 sec	Florence Griffith Joyner	16 Jul 1988	0.0 m/sec
100 m hurdles	12.21 sec	Yordanka Dankova	20 Aug 1988	0.7 m/sec tailwind
Long jump	7.52 m	Galina Christyakova	11 Jun 1988	1.4 m/sec tailwind
Triple jump	15.50 m	Inessa Kravets	10 Aug 1995	0.9 m/sec tailwind

One way to get a better feel for how chance events affect contest outcomes is to perform numerical simulations that examine a range of assumptions about the extent to which luck influences performance. Numerical simulations are widely used in both the social and physical sciences to help researchers better understand complex interactive processes.

Consider again the earlier question of how likely it is that you'd get heads 20 consecutive times when flipping a fair coin.

For someone trained in basic probability theory, it's straightforward to calculate this likelihood directly.[3] But for many complex problems, explicit solutions aren't feasible. In such cases, an alternative way to proceed would be to simulate the assumed conditions a large number of times and observe how often the event happens. For the coin-flip example, we might assign an army of volunteers to do 20 consecutive coin flips a billion times, and then estimate the likelihood of getting heads 20 times as the proportion of those billion trials that actually resulted in 20 heads.

Of course, it wouldn't make sense to enlist volunteers to perform actual coin flips, since a computer could easily be programmed to replicate the pattern of outcomes we'd expect to see in a process like that. That's essentially the approach I'm taking to get a feel for how important luck is in determining who will prevail in a winner-take-all contest with a large number of contestants.

In appendix 1, I describe a number of simulations of such contests. Like track and field events, all take the form of a winner-take-all tournament whose outcome depends only on performance. Performance is objectively measurable, and whichever contestant has the highest total performance score wins the contest. Performance, in turn, depends in varying degrees on talent, effort, and luck.

One of the simulations examines a baseline case with 100,000 contestants and in which luck counts for only 2 percent of total performance. The remaining 98 percent is accounted for in equal parts by ability and effort. Each contestant's ability, effort, and luck values are independently drawn random numbers that are equally likely to lie anywhere between 0 and 100. The average luck score of contest winners in that simulation is 90.23, and 78.1 percent of winners did *not* have the highest combined total of talent and effort values. In most of those cases, there were several others with higher combined talent and effort values than the winner's.

If luck has only a very small effect on performance, why is it so hard to win a large contest unless you're very lucky? Two factors are involved. One is that the inherent randomness of luck means that the most skilled contestant is no more likely to be lucky than anyone else. The second factor is that with a large number of contestants, there are bound to be many with close to the maximum skill level, and among those at least some will also happen to be very lucky. With very large contestant pools, then, there will almost always be someone who is almost as skillful as the most talented contestant, but is also significantly luckier. So even when luck counts for only a tiny fraction of total performance, the winner of a large contest will seldom be the most skillful contestant, but will usually be one of the luckiest.

The simulations described in appendix 1 also help us understand both the strengths and weaknesses of the human capital approach discussed earlier. People who achieve material success on a grand scale will almost always be both highly talented and extremely hardworking, just as the human capital approach suggests. But the simulations also make clear, in a way the human capital approach does not, why so many extremely talented and hardworking people fail to achieve any significant measure of material success. Many of them are simply less lucky than the winners.

If the simulations challenge our intuitions about the importance of chance events, it's at least in part because we sense, correctly, that performance depends far more strongly on ability and effort than on small random occurrences. Our intuitions often fail because even things that are highly improbable in any specific instance become likely if there are enough opportunities for them to occur.

Most of the things that happen in most of our lives are of course not the least bit strange. Yet in almost everyone's life, at least some strange things have happened. My late Cornell colleague Carl Sagan described a vivid dream he'd once had in which a close relative had died. When he called home, he was relieved to learn that his relative was still in good health. But Sagan went on to observe that there must be millions of people who at one time or another have a vivid dream about a loved one dying. And by chance alone, some small number of those loved ones will have actually died during that same night.[4]

Sagan was a lifelong skeptic about supernatural events. But he conceded that if his loved one had in fact died during the night of his dream, he would have found it difficult to believe it a mere coincidence—notwithstanding his awareness that such unlikely conjunctions of events are bound to happen to someone.

It's no mystery that astonishingly improbable events have the power to, well, astonish. I was not naïve to have been astonished upon learning that the classmate with whom my newly discovered sister had grown up in a Virginia hamlet was living across the street from me in Ithaca decades later. The odds of such a thing happening to *me* were of course just as remote as they seemed.

But the likelihood of something similar happening to *someone, somewhere*, is not small at all. Because we live a long time and because there are so many of us, such events are bound to happen.

If performance depends almost entirely on ability and effort, our intuitions tell us that those with the most talent and drive will almost inevitably prevail. Those intuitions are strongly supported by the observation that the winners in highly competitive arenas almost always are, in fact, highly driven and talented people.

But let luck matter in even the most trivial ways and our intuitions begin to unravel. The contests that determine society's biggest economic winners invariably attract an enormous number of contestants. Many if not most of them will be enormously talented and energetic. In most cases, however, those who prevail would not have done so if they had not also been unusually lucky.

Again, I emphasize that this isn't the same as saying that most winners win *only* because they're lucky. In highly competitive arenas, most would not have even been realistic contenders had they not been both extremely able and hardworking. It would be grossly unfair, then, to say that most winners didn't deserve their rewards. It is no stretch, for example, to call Bryan Cranston one of today's most deservedly successful dramatic actors, even though no one would describe him that way if John Cusack and Matthew Broderick hadn't turned down the Walter White role in *Breaking Bad* before Cranston was offered it. Cranston, to his credit, seems fully cognizant of his good fortune. "Luck," he said, "is a component that a lot of people in the arts sometimes fail to recognize: that you can have talent, perseverance, patience, but without luck you will not have a successful career."[5]

5
♠

WHY FALSE BELIEFS ABOUT
LUCK AND TALENT PERSIST

In his 2012 book, *The Success Equation*, Michael Mauboussin describes a man inspired by a succession of dreams to believe he'd win the Spanish National Lottery if he could purchase a ticket number whose last two digits were 48. After an extensive search, he located and bought such a ticket, which indeed turned out to be a winner. When an interviewer later asked why he'd sought out that particular number, he said, "I dreamed of the number 7 for seven straight nights. And 7 times 7 is 48."[1]

Mauboussin's lottery player doesn't summon images of the disciplined, rational actors who populate traditional economic models. Those models have enhanced our understanding of human behavior and social institutions, to be sure, but they also fail to capture much of the craziness we see around us. That's why behavioral economics—a cross-disciplinary effort that draws insights from economics, psychology, biology, and other fields—has been the most vibrant and rapidly growing specialty in economics for the past three decades.

Inspired by the pioneering work of the psychologists Daniel Kahneman and the late Amos Tversky, this field has cataloged a large inventory of behavioral anomalies in which people clearly violate the predictions and prescriptions of standard economic models.[2] It is common, for example, for someone to be willing to drive across town to save $10 on a $20 clock radio, but unwilling to do so to save $10 on a $1,000 television set. Yet the benefit of making the drive is $10 in each case. So if the implicit cost of the drive were less than $10, a rational person would drive across town in both cases. People often explain their reluctance to make the drive for the television by saying the $10 savings is such a small percentage of its price. But a rational person reckons benefits and costs in absolute terms, not as percentages. As Tversky, then a professor of psychology at Stanford University, was said to have quipped, "My colleagues, they study artificial intelligence. Me? I study natural stupidity."

Much of the work in behavioral economics rests on people's tendency to rely on mental shortcuts or rules of thumb. These rules are largely adaptive in the sense that the time and effort they save more than compensate for the possibility that they're somewhat less accurate than more detailed calculations. Although heuristics work reasonably well much of the time, they also produce systematic errors in judgment and attribution in some contexts.

For present purposes, of special interest is how behavioral research has informed our thinking about the tendency to hold persistent false beliefs. Why, for example, do many more than half of us believe ourselves to be in the top half of any given talent distribution? And why do so many of us downplay luck's importance in the face of compelling evidence to the contrary? One plausible explanation, I'll argue, is that people with more realistic beliefs about their talents and about luck's importance may actually find it more difficult to muster the will to overcome the difficult obstacles that litter every path to success.

The economist Paul Samuelson once said, "Never underestimate the willingness of a man to believe flattering things about himself." Samuelson was not a behavioral economist, but he clearly recognized that people's self-assessments were often higher than warranted by objective evidence. In surveys, for example, more than 90 percent of people describe themselves as above-average drivers. The same self-assessment was reported by more than 80 percent of drivers surveyed while they were in the hospital recovering from accidents, many of which they had surely caused themselves.

It's of course possible for most people to have a trait that measures higher than the corresponding mean value for the population to which they belong. Since a small number of people have fewer than two legs and no one has more, for instance, the average number of legs in any human population is slightly less than two. So most people actually do have "more legs than average."

But it's difficult even to imagine how we might define, much less calculate, a quantitative measure of average driving skill. So in calling themselves "above-average drivers," survey respondents more likely meant that they were "more skillful than the median driver." That would of course be impossible in the aggregate, since only half the people in any distribution can be in the top half.

In any event, it's easy to find examples of cases in which we embrace implausible beliefs about how good we are. Almost 70 percent of the faculty surveyed at one university believed themselves to be in the top 25 percent of their colleagues with respect to teaching ability.[3] And another survey found that 87 percent of students in an elite MBA program believed their academic performance placed them in the top half of their class.[4]

This pattern has been called the Lake Wobegon Effect, after Garrison Keillor's mythical Minnesota small town where "all the children are above average." The pattern is typically more pronounced for traits or characteristics that are difficult to measure objectively, such as driving ability. Only 2 percent of high school students in one survey said they had below-average leadership ability, and virtually all rated themselves as better than average at getting along with others.[5]

False beliefs about luck are also common. Lottery winners, for example, sometimes offer detailed accounts of how various personal skills and insights enabled them to pick their winning numbers.[6] In a 1991 paper, Charles Clotfelter and Philip Cook described popular books that advise people how to choose lottery numbers on the basis of things that appear in their dreams. One such book, *Prince Ali Lucky Five Star*, which they purchased from a vendor near Harvard Yard, counseled playing 416 in the wake of dreams about apples, 305 after dreams about bugs, 999 after those about graves, and 001 for dreams involving priests.[7]

Yet as anyone familiar with the random number generators that spit out winning lottery numbers knows, efforts to forecast those numbers are in vain. The algorithms are designed to ensure that all possible numbers are equally likely to come up. People continue, however, to imagine they possess skills or insights that can command an edge.

Another disconnect between evidence and belief is people's tendency to underestimate good fortune's role in success, while being too quick to embrace bad luck as an explanation of failure. The statistician Nassim Taleb, for example, describes this tendency as common among investors.[8] Some have attributed it to so-called motivated cognition: People want to feel good about themselves, and they're more likely to enjoy the warm glow of a positive self-image if they think of themselves as highly competent and attribute their failures to events beyond their control.

In a 1979 paper subtitled "Sadder but Wiser," the psychologists L. B. Alloy and L. Y. Abramson provided some support for this theory.[9] Alloy and Abramson challenged the then conventional view that depressed people suffered from cognitive biases that led them to embrace unrealistically negative beliefs about the world and themselves.[10] In place of that theory, they offered their "depressive realism" hypothesis, according to which the assessments of depressed persons were actually more accurate than those of ostensibly normal people.

This hypothesis was spawned by experiments comparing the self-assessments of a group of clinically depressed students with those of a control group not suffering from depression. Subjects in each group were asked to perform a variety of tasks and then rate themselves on how well they had done. The self-assessments of the depressed students closely tracked the assessments made by external observers. But the nondepressed students consistently overestimated the quality of their own performance in tasks at which they succeeded, and underestimated · the importance of their own performance in tasks in which they performed poorly.[11]

This paper stimulated considerable discussion, and there is still no robust consensus about its findings. But even those who interpret those findings to imply that holding false beliefs makes people happier in the short run will want to remain open to the possibility that such beliefs may entail significant costs longer term.

That possibility is underscored by Charles Darwin's insight that natural selection did not forge our nervous systems to make us happy, but rather to spur behaviors that promote survival and reproduction. People who believe they're destined to win any contest they enter may enter many contests they shouldn't, incurring costs they could have avoided. Those who are overly prone to attribute their failures to bad luck may be unreceptive to the kinds of feedback needed to improve future performance. Neither of these tendencies appears likely to promote reproductive success.

So even if inaccurate beliefs tend to make people happier, those happy people might have been a little more successful, in purely material terms, if their beliefs had tracked the truth more closely. A related possibility, which I'll consider in the next chapter, is that more accurate beliefs about skill and luck could increase support for public policies that would enhance everyone's prospects for material success in the long run.

Notwithstanding such possibilities, there may be cases in which holding false beliefs could be adaptive. The economist Michael Manove describes a plausible example. When asked to serve as his department's vice-chairman, he followed the economist's standard drill, comparing his estimates of the relevant costs and benefits of the position. Most prominent on the benefit side was the job's annual stipend of several thousand dollars. Manove decided to accept the post because his estimate of how much he'd be willing to pay to avoid its inevitable hassles was smaller than the stipend.

Once he'd been in the job for a while, however, he realized that he'd been a victim of what economists call the winner's curse. In any auction, different bidders have different estimates of the value of the thing on offer, some higher than its true value, others lower. But even if all estimates are unbiased, so that the average of the estimates is close to the thing's true value, the highest bidder will tend to be the one whose estimate exceeds the true value by the largest amount. Manove views his decision to accept his department's vice-chairmanship as a consequence of his having underestimated the hassles of the post by a wider margin than his colleagues did.[12]

But he went on to note that although accepting the job made him less happy than his colleagues, it also made him wealthier. And in the Darwinian struggle for survival, what you have matters more than how happy you are. According to Manove, the moral of his experience was that naïve optimism, within limits, can be adaptive.

If people had realistic estimates of the magnitude of the hassles they'd face upon starting their own business, few would have the courage to go forward. But having launched such ventures, people typically do everything within their power to make them succeed. Most of those who make it may thus owe their good fortune in part to naïve optimism.

What about false beliefs about luck? If, as I claim, chance events are becoming more important, why do so many people still insist they don't matter? By emphasizing talent and hard work to the exclusion of other factors, successful people may be trying to reinforce their claim to the money they've earned. I'll have more to say about that possibility in the next chapter. Here I'll explore a more charitable view, which is that denying the importance of luck may actually help people summon the formidable efforts generally required for success.

One of the biggest obstacles to success is a simple feature of human psychology: the tendency to give too little weight to events that occur with either uncertainty or delay. Many researchers have argued that self-control problems often lead people to choose immediately available rewards, even in the face of far more valuable alternatives that require waiting.[13]

Researchers have invoked this tendency to explain a laundry list of ills that plague modern societies. In their 2011 book, *Willpower*,[14] the psychologist Roy Baumeister and the science writer John Tierney surveyed voluminous and persuasive evidence that self-control deficits underlie such diverse problems as "addiction, overeating, crime, domestic violence, sexually transmitted diseases, prejudice, debt, unwanted pregnancy, educational failure, underperformance at school and work, [and] lack of exercise."[15]

A tendency to emphasize current costs and benefits may have been advantageous in environments in which people faced immediate threats to their survival. Far better, perhaps, to focus all of one's attention on such challenges than to spend time and energy planning for a future that might otherwise never come. But in the more stable environments that characterize most wealthy societies today, caring only about immediate costs and benefits is a recipe for failure.

Consider students who want to attend an elite university to improve their job prospects upon graduation. Because the battle for admission to top schools has grown so competitive, they won't even be considered unless they have exceptional grades and test scores. But not even the smartest students can earn better grades than their talented classmates without considerable effort. And getting top scores on admissions tests often requires long hours of intensive study complemented by expensive and tedious professional coaching.

Those efforts have to happen now, or better still, to have begun years earlier. In contrast, the corresponding rewards come only with many years of delay, if they come at all. That disparity strongly discourages current effort, even when the potential future rewards are enormous. Because the costs of taking an action are vivid and immediate, they spring quickly to mind. But if the benefits of acting are delayed, they must be imagined. It's thus no mystery that many students avoid the painful steps required to gain admission to highly selective universities.

This temptation becomes greater when future rewards appear less certain. A narrative that openly acknowledges the strong link between success and luck calls explicit attention to this uncertainty. It might thus discourage the very efforts that are so often critical for success.

And hence the paradox inherent in denying luck's importance: Parents who teach their children that luck doesn't matter may for that very reason be more likely to raise successful children than parents who tell their children the truth. When the going gets tough, as it inevitably does along almost every career path, someone who's keenly sensitive to luck's importance may be more tempted just to sit back and see what happens.

In competitive environments, where genuine expertise is often an essential precondition for success, that's a horrible strategy. In almost any field, thousands of hours of hard practice are required to become an expert.[16] Hard practice means repeatedly trying and failing before managing to achieve even marginal extensions of skills that you haven't yet mastered. It's generally difficult to summon the effort to do that. If you're focused on luck's importance, you may be more likely to think of excuses to avoid that effort and instead hope that fate will intervene on your behalf. So if believing that talent and effort are all that matter makes it easier to tackle difficult tasks, then denying luck's importance may be adaptive.

The findings of attribution theory in psychology offer additional support for the possibility that denying luck's role in success may spur additional effort.[17] It's been shown, for instance, that students are more likely to persist with difficult academic tasks if they view any resulting success as having stemmed primarily from their own abilities and efforts.[18] Given that high ability is a persistent personal trait, such beliefs encourage continued hard work in the future. Embracing effort as a cause of success makes sense for similar reasons, since it's under one's own control and could hence be recruited to promote future success.

Similar reasoning suggests why attitudes about luck's role in failure also matter, but in the opposite way. If past failures are viewed as having resulted from bad luck, there's no presumption that future endeavors will be similarly handicapped, and thus no reason to avoid trying hard when new opportunities arise.[19]

Parallel issues arise in discussions of free will. Some believe that every human action is determined by prior events, that free will is essentially an illusion. Others insist that when we confront a fork in the road, we always have the power to choose either path, even though external factors—such as genes, experience, diets, and other influences—may make a particular choice more likely.

Given our still limited understanding of how human brains actually function, this debate won't be settled soon. For present purposes, however, that may not matter much. Even if it could be shown, for example, that a murderer's actions were completely determined by prior events, we would still find it prudent to punish murderers, since people would be less likely to kill if they knew they'd be held accountable. At the same time, we're often willing to grant judges considerable discretion in sentencing, knowing that they'll exercise it when they think defendants aren't fully responsible for their actions.

Given the similarity of the underlying issues involved, it's perhaps no surprise that people's disagreements about the penal code tend to mimic their disagreements about luck. Those who are more likely to embrace luck's importance are also more likely to accept childhood disadvantage as a mitigating factor in adult misconduct.[20]

Suppose, for the sake of argument, that neuroscientists were someday successful in demonstrating that free will doesn't exist, and that every future choice could in fact be predicted accurately from current information. Would such knowledge help people deal with tough decisions? It's difficult to see how. At any rate, there is evidence from laboratory settings that people who are tempted by an immediate but inferior reward are more likely to succumb if they believe that their choices are preordained.[21] As with beliefs about luck, then, beliefs about free will might be adaptive even if they are objectively false.

Our understanding of human cognition suggests additional reasons for the tendency to underestimate luck's role in success. One of the rules of thumb people often use when making judgments is the so-called availability heuristic. Suppose you're asked, "Which are more frequent: English words that start with the letter 'R,' or those that have 'R' as their third letter?" Using the availability heuristic, most people react by trying to think of examples in each category. That approach usually works well, since examples of things that occur more frequently are in fact generally easier to summon from memory. And since most people find it easier to think of examples of words starting with "R," the availability heuristic leads them to answer that such words occur more frequently. Yet English words with "R" in the third slot are actually far more numerous.

The availability heuristic fails here because frequency isn't the only thing that governs ease of recall. We store words in our memories in multiple ways—by their meanings, by the sounds they make and the images they evoke, by their first letters, and by numerous other features. But virtually no one stores words in memory by the identity of their third letter.

The availability heuristic suggests that when we construct narratives about how the world works, we rely more heavily on information that happens to be more accessible from memory. But that almost guarantees that our accounts will be biased, since some types of information are far more readily accessible than others. Information about things we've experienced repeatedly, for example, is far more salient than information about things we've only heard or read about infrequently. Information in the latter category has a much harder time breaking through.

Little wonder, then, that when smart, hardworking people strike it rich, it's completely natural for them to ascribe their success to talent and hard work alone. Most of them, after all, are vividly aware of how hard they've worked and how talented they are. They've been working hard and solving difficult problems every day for many years!

They probably also know, in some abstract sense, that they might not have done as well in some other environments. Yet their day-to-day experiences provide only infrequent reminders to reflect on how fortunate they were not to have been born in, say, a war-torn country like Zimbabwe.

The availability heuristic biases our personal narratives in a second way, because events that work to our disadvantage are systematically easier to recall than those that affect us positively. My Cornell colleague Tom Gilovich invokes a metaphor involving headwinds and tailwinds to describe this asymmetry.

> If any of you go running or ride a bike, you'll know that when you're running or bicycling into the wind, you're very aware of it. You just can't wait till the course turns around and you've got the wind at your back. When that happens, you feel *great*. But then you forget about it very quickly—you're just not aware of the wind at your back. And that's just a fundamental feature of how our minds work. We're just going to be more aware of those barriers than of the things that boost us along.[22]

Even bicyclists who benefit from a tailwind often experience themselves as riding into the wind. Someone riding 12 mph in the same direction as an 8 mph wind, for instance, would actually experience a 4 mph wind in his face.

Gilovich notes that a Google image search on "headwind" serves up numerous images like this that capture the concept vividly:

Headwinds: easy to illustrate.

But an image search on "tailwind" turns up very different results. As Gilovich explains,

> You have to depict [the concept] schematically, you just can't capture it in an image. And what's true photographically is also true psychologically. That is to say, since we're goal-striving, problem-solving organisms, we're naturally going to be oriented towards the barriers that we have to overcome.... We readily spot the advantages others enjoy (that we don't) and the difficulties we face (that others don't), meanwhile merrily blind to our own advantages and the tribulations of others. And, being the jumping-to-conclusions machines that we are, we're prone to weaving the evidence into a "victim me"/"deserving me" narrative.[23]

Gilovich and his coauthor Shai Davidai further illustrate the headwinds/tailwinds asymmetry by surveying people who have just completed rounds of Wordical, a Scrabble-like game in which each player uses letters drawn at random to make words. As in all such games, the more skillful player in any pair will win more often in the long run. But in any given round, a less skillful player can get lucky, defeating a more skillful opponent by drawing better letters. The researchers asked participants to identify the five best letters and the five worst letters in the game (in terms of the tradeoff between letters that are easy to use in making words but score few points, and those with the opposite properties). Participants were then asked to estimate the relative frequencies of the extreme letters drawn in each category, both by themselves and by their opponents. Since there are five letters of each type, we expect a 50–50 split on the average. Players estimated that they personally had drawn a roughly equal number of extreme letters of each type, consistent with that expectation. Yet they also believed that 56 percent of the letters drawn by their opponents had been in the best category—effectively overestimating their opponents' shares of the best letters by more than 10 percent.[24]

Exactly half of participants emerge as winners of this game, the remaining half as losers. And since players believe, on average, that their opponents had drawn more favorable letters, winners appear to believe, at least implicitly, that their superior skill enabled them to prevail in spite of their opponents' good luck.

That we tend to overestimate our own responsibility for whatever successes we've enjoyed in life is not to say that we shouldn't take pride in our accomplishments, even those that would never have occurred without the help of lucky breaks or other external events. That's because pride in one's achievements is often one of the most powerful motivations to expend the effort it takes to succeed.

It's also perfectly intelligible that most of us feel entitled to credit for possessing skills we did nothing to earn. Some months ago, a graduate student I had taught during the 1980s asked me to comment on a health policy article he'd written. He and I had played together on the department's softball team, and his e-mail message contained this sentence: "I recall you as not only a great teacher, but perhaps possessing the best throwing arm I have ever seen on a softball field!" There might have been some logic in the pleasure I took at being remembered as a good teacher, since I had invested significant effort in my courses. But I can't say the same about the warm glow provoked by his comment about my throwing arm.

That wasn't a skill I'd developed through any effort. The fact that I could always throw a ball farther than any of my classmates was just an accident of DNA. Yet that realization did little to stifle the stupid delight I experienced upon reading that sentence. That's apparently just the way the human psyche is constituted. And it may be a good thing, since those who take delight in being good at something, whether earned or not, are more likely to find arenas in which they can compete successfully.

Laboratory studies by psychologists support the popular wisdom that liberals are more likely than conservatives to embrace the importance of luck in life.[25] But there are numerous exceptions to this pattern, and the differences between opposing views are often far more nuanced than popular accounts suggest. David Brooks, the right-of-center op-ed columnist at the New York Times, captured the middle ground nicely in a piece published during the 2012 presidential campaign. He began by quoting from a letter he said he'd received from an Ohio businessman:

Dear Mr. Opinion Guy,

Over the past few years, I've built a successful business. I've worked hard, and I'm proud of what I've done. But now President Obama tells me that social and political forces helped build that. Mitt Romney went to Israel and said cultural forces explain the differences in the wealth of nations. I'm confused. How much of my success is me, and how much of my success comes from forces outside of me?

Confused in Columbus

Brooks responded that the best way to think about the role of external forces depends on where you are in the life cycle and on whether you're looking ahead or back. His specific advice to Confused in Columbus:

You should regard yourself as the sole author of all your future achievements and as the grateful beneficiary of all your past successes.... As you go through life, you should pass through different phases in thinking about how much credit you deserve. You should start your life with the illusion that you are completely in control of what you do. You should finish life with the recognition that, all in all, you got better than you deserved.... As an ambitious executive, it's important that you believe that you will deserve credit for everything you achieve. As a human being, it's important for you to know that's nonsense.

Spot on, Mr. Brooks!

As F. Scott Fitzgerald observed, "The test of a first-rate intelligence is the ability to hold two opposing ideas in mind at the same time and still retain the ability to function." By that test, clear thinking about luck demands an extremely high level of intelligence, for it requires that we embrace the starkly contradictory views on the subject held by people at different points along the political spectrum. But the challenge is made a little less daunting by the fact that both views incorporate essential elements of the truth.

6
♠

THE BURDEN OF FALSE BELIEFS

If you share my view that material prosperity is a good thing, there is one dimension of personal luck that transcends all others, which is to have been born in a highly developed country. No matter how talented and ambitious you may be, material success is only a remote possibility in the world's poorest countries.

Recall my description of Birkhaman Rai, the young Bhutanese hill tribesman who worked as my cook long ago during my stay as a Peace Corps volunteer in Nepal. Because he didn't know how to read or write, I couldn't keep in touch with him after returning to the United States, but I've often wondered what became of him. He was as talented and resourceful as anyone I've ever known, yet he probably never managed to earn even the meager average Nepalese income, currently somewhat less than $1,500 a year.

If he'd been born here, he'd almost surely be a highly prosperous, perhaps even very wealthy, man today. If he's still alive, he would be in his seventies, well past the normal life expectancy for men in Nepal. Had he been born here, however, he could expect many more years of good health and prosperity.

Of course, individuals can't choose the environments into which they're born. But society as a whole can mold those environments in significant ways. Doing so, however, requires intensive levels of investment. We who were born into highly developed countries are thus the lucky beneficiaries of centuries of intensive investment by those who came before us.

In recent decades, however, those investments have been depreciating. A 2013 report from the American Society of Civil Engineers estimated that the United States faced a $3.6 trillion backlog in essential maintenance for existing infrastructure.[1] Crumbling roads and unsafe bridges are common across the country, as are failing water and sewage systems. Millions live downstream from dams that could collapse at any moment. Countless school buildings are in disrepair.

We've also done little to expand and improve existing infrastructure. Morocco, a country whose per capita income is roughly a tenth that of the United States, is nearing completion of a 350-kilometer high-speed rail link between Casablanca and Tangier. Trains along much of that line will travel at 200 mph. In the United States, which has one of the world's most densely populated rail corridors, proposals to build high-speed rail consistently fail in Congress. The fastest trains along our northeast corridor average only 80 mph.

Even more troubling, support for public education has diminished sharply in recent decades. Using revenue and spending data from the National Center for Education Statistics' Delta Cost Project Database,[2] one carefully documented study estimates that reduced state funding accounted for roughly 80 percent of the past decade's more than $3,000 increase in average annual tuition at public four-year universities.[3] More than 70 percent of students graduating from four-year colleges in 2014 had student loan balances that averaged $33,000.[4]

More troubling still has been the pattern of reduced investment on behalf of children in low-income households. The parents of children higher up the income ladder have the means to compensate for budget and program cutbacks that have been occurring in the public schools. They can send their children to private schools, or pay for private music lessons, athletic coaching, and SAT prep courses. Or they can enroll their children in pay-for-play programs in the public schools. Those options are beyond reach for low-income households.

Many factors have contributed to our failure to maintain historic levels of public investment, but one in particular stands out: Citizens' demands for government services have outstripped government tax revenue. That phenomenon, in turn, has many causes, among them the sharply rising costs of health care and pensions associated with our aging population.

But an additional contributing factor, as the entries in table 6.1 suggest, has been a long-term decline in our top marginal tax

TABLE 6.1. MAXIMUM MARGINAL TAX RATES ON INDIVIDUAL INCOME

	1979	1990	2002
Argentina	45	30	35
Australia	62	48	47
Austria	62	50	50
Belgium	76	55	52
Brazil	55	25	28
Canada (Ontario)	58	47	46
Denmark	73	68	59
Egypt	80	65	40
France	60	52	50

	1979	1990	2002
Germany	56	53	49
Greece	60	50	40
Hong Kong	25*	25	16
India	60	50	30
Ireland	65	56	42
Israel	66	48	50
Italy	72	50	52
Japan	75	50	50
South Korea	89	50	36
Mexico	55	35	40
Netherlands	72	60	52
New Zealand	60	33	39
Norway	75	54	48
Portugal	84	40	40
Puerto Rico	79	43	33
Singapore	55	33	26
Spain	66	56	48
Sweden	87	65	56
Turkey	75	50	45
United Kingdom	83	40	40
United States	70	33	39

Source: PricewaterhouseCoopers; International Bureau of Fiscal Documentation
*Hong Kong's maximum tax (the "standard rate") has normally been 15 percent, effectively capping the marginal rate at high income levels (in exchange for no personal exemptions).

rates—a trend that has occurred in many countries around the globe. Many tax cuts were adopted in the hope that they would stimulate economic growth by enough to prevent a decline in overall tax revenues, but it hasn't worked out that way. The nonpartisan Congressional Budget Office estimated that the effect of the George W. Bush tax cuts was to reduce federal revenue by $2.9 trillion between 2001 and 2011. And in a widely cited *New York Times* article, Bruce Bartlett, a senior economic advisor in the administrations of Ronald Reagan and George H. W. Bush, argued that the actual revenue shortfall caused by the Bush tax cuts was considerably larger.[5] If Bartlett is right, that shortfall would have been enough to eliminate our current estimated infrastructure backlog.

If being born in a good environment is one of the luckiest things that can happen to anyone, it is failure to appreciate luck's importance that has done the most to undermine our collective stock of good fortune. That's because failure to appreciate luck's importance has made successful people more reluctant to pay the taxes required to support the investments necessary to maintain a good environment. As we'll see, more realistic beliefs about luck would not only make it easier to create and maintain environments that would sustain the luck of future generations; they would also improve the material living standards of even society's most successful members.

But first a word about the meaning of "improved material living standards." Many interpret the expression to mean "having more stuff." But it really means something much more general, which is being able to achieve more fully all the goals we care about. That might include having more stuff, but it would also include having cleaner air, safer streets, more time to spend with family and friends, and a host of other valuable intangibles.

No one disputes that a mix of both public and private consumption is necessary for people to achieve basic goals. As noted in chapter 1, for example, cars are of little use without roads, and roads are of little use without cars. But there is much disagreement about what constitutes the most desirable mix of public and private consumption. The fact that Americans are driving the best cars ever produced on roads that are riddled with potholes suggests that our current balance between cars and roads is far from optimal. Because additional expenditures on cars, beyond some point, produce only marginal improvements in performance, we could spend less on cars without giving up much of value, freeing up money that could better maintain the roads. The result would be a significant improvement in the overall driving experience of almost every motorist. No matter how wealthy you were, you'd probably prefer driving a $150,000 Porsche 911 Turbo on a well-maintained highway to driving a $333,000 Ferrari Berlinetta on a pothole-ridden road. So why do so many wealthy drivers continue to favor lower taxes, even knowing that means further degradation of the nation's infrastructure?

This strange posture, I believe, is explained by a combination of two cognitive errors. One is the seemingly plausible, but essentially false, belief that higher taxes would make it significantly harder to buy what they want. The other is the tendency, discussed in the preceding chapter, for successful people to underestimate the importance of luck in their own lives. Both errors make it more difficult to perceive and appreciate the possible attractions of high-quality public services financed by higher taxes. I'll consider them in turn.

The first error was on vivid display during a lunchtime conversation several years ago with one of my colleagues. When he asked whether I'd heard about all the new taxes that President Obama had in store for us and I said that I hadn't, he expressed shock at my ignorance. I explained that it just didn't make sense for people like us to worry about such things. When he asked why, I began by confirming that he agreed with me that there was no chance the government would enact tax changes that would threaten our ability to buy what we needed. (He and I are both authors of widely adopted textbooks, which in a town like Ithaca means we don't spend nearly as much as we earn.)

I then asked whether he was worried that higher taxes would make us less able to buy what we wanted. Yes, that was exactly his worry! But since all our basic needs have already been met, the kinds of things that people like us want are mostly things that there aren't enough of—say, a house with a commanding view of the lake, or a choice slip in the marina. To get such things, we have to outbid other people like us who also want them, people with similar tastes and incomes. So if the government raises our taxes, the taxes of those other people go up, too. And that leaves the bidding wars that determine who gets the things we want essentially unaffected. The best home sites and marina slips go to the same people as before.

In short, the effects of a decline in any one person's after-tax income are dramatically different from those of an across-the-board decline. If you alone experience an income decline, you're less able to buy what you want. But when everyone's income declines simultaneously, relative purchasing power is unaffected. And it's relative purchasing power that determines who gets things that are in short supply.

Since the vast majority of income declines that people experience—whether from the loss of a job or a divorce or a home fire—are losses that affect only them, the availability heuristic leads us to think of higher taxes as being just like other income losses. If you lose your job, you really *are* less able to bid successfully for a home with a view. But when everyone's disposable income declines—as happens when taxes rise—it's a totally different story.

Like the failure to appreciate the distinction between unilateral and across-the-board income declines, underestimating the importance of luck is also a totally understandable tendency. As discussed earlier, when smart, hardworking people strike it rich, it's natural for them to ascribe their success to talent and hard work alone.

Both cognitive errors also make it more difficult to raise the revenue needed to sustain the environments we were lucky to be born into. That's because overlooking luck's role makes those who've succeeded at the highest levels feel much more entitled to keep the lion's share of the income they've earned.

One piece of evidence for this claim comes from laboratory experiments involving bargaining games that are played between strangers. One version, the "ultimatum game," has two players, the proposer and the responder. The proposer is given a sum of money—say $100—and told to propose a division of it between himself and the responder. Any combination that adds up to $100 is allowed, provided the responder is offered at least $1. The responder can then either accept the offer, in which case the money is distributed as proposed; or he can reject it, in which case the $100 goes back to the experimenter and each player gets zero. The two players interact only once, ruling out the possibility of establishing a reputation for being a tough bargainer.

If each player were purely self-interested, the optimal move for the proposer would be to offer $1 to the responder and take the remaining $99 for himself. A purely self-interested responder would accept this offer, realizing that a dollar was better than nothing.

In thousands of replications of this experiment, however, most proposers don't offer such one-sided splits. Many, in fact, make 50–50 offers. That might reflect concerns about fairness or generosity, but it could also result from fear that responders would reject highly uneven splits. And sure enough, in the small minority of cases in which proposers do make extremely one-sided offers, rejections are common.

One variant of this experiment allows us to focus specifically on false beliefs about luck.[6] As before, there is a proposer and a responder who must divide a given sum of money. But this time both players are first shown a computer screen with a large and apparently almost equal number of dots distributed on either side of a vertical line. They are asked whether there are more dots to the right or left side of the line, and then receive one of four possible combinations of feedback: both players answered correctly, both players answered incorrectly, the proposer was correct while the responder was incorrect, or the proposer was incorrect while the responder was correct. Unbeknownst to the players, the feedback is actually randomly generated and bears no relationship to either player's true performance. In short, the players are led to believe that the results reflect their respective skill levels, but in fact they are purely random.

As expected, the researchers found that when players were told that the proposer was correct and the responder was incorrect, proposers went on to make significantly more one-sided offers in their own favor, which responders were significantly more likely to accept. The reverse was true when players were told that the proposer was incorrect and the responder was correct. But the differences in behavior were highly asymmetric. When proposers were told that they were correct and the responder was incorrect, they claimed a much larger share of the total for themselves than when they were told that both had performed equally well. But when proposers were told that they were incorrect and the responder was correct, they proposed only a little less for themselves than when they were told that both had performed equally well. Falsely believing themselves to be more skillful apparently induced a powerful sense of entitlement to claim the lion's share, while falsely believing themselves to be less skillful had much less of an effect.

My very able research assistant Yuezhou Huo designed a simple survey that sheds additional light on how focusing on the importance of external factors can affect people's willingness to contribute to the common good. She began by asking subjects recruited online from Amazon's Mechanical Turk worker pool[7] to recall a good thing that had recently happened to them. She then asked one group to list external factors beyond their control that contributed to the event, a second group to list personal qualities or things they had done personally, and a control group to simply list reasons that the good thing had happened.

Subjects in each group were paid 50 cents for signing up and promised an additional $1 for completing the experiment. At the end of the experiment, she offered subjects in each of the three groups an opportunity to donate part or all of the additional $1 to one of three charities (their choice among Planned Parenthood, the World Wildlife Fund, and Doctors without Borders).

As shown in figure 6.1, subjects who'd been asked to recall a good event and come up with external causes—many of whom mentioned luck explicitly, or cited factors like supportive spouses, thoughtful teachers, and financial aid—gave more than 25 percent larger donations than those who'd been asked to offer internal causes to explain the good event. Members of that group mentioned factors like hard work, determination, and careful decision making. The donations of subjects in the control group were roughly midway between the other two. As we'll presently see, these findings are consistent with those in a large body of research by academic psychologists who have studied how the emotion of gratitude affects people's behavior.

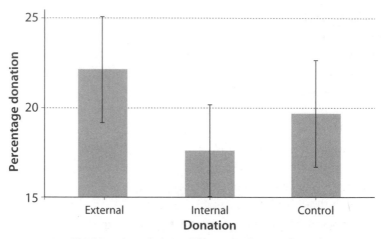

FIGURE 6.1. Thinking about their good fortune makes people more generous. External: Mean = 22.14, Number of subjects = 93; Internal: Mean = 17.61, Number of subjects = 108; Control: Mean = 19.67, Number of subjects = 100.

Failure to recognize luck's role in success may also increase reluctance to pay taxes by reinforcing the natural sense of entitlement to income produced by the fruits of one's own labor. As the seventeenth-century British philosopher John Locke wrote, "every man has a property in his own person. This nobody has any right to but himself. The labour of his body, and the work of his hands, we may say, are properly his."[8] With these words, Locke became the patron saint of tax resisters around the world.

This sense of entitlement to the fruits of one's labors may owe much to the phenomenon known as loss aversion. One of the most reliable findings in behavioral economics, loss aversion refers to the fact that people will fight much harder to avoid a loss than they would to achieve a gain of the same amount.[9] Since most successful people work extremely hard for the money they earn, it *feels* like they own it, and that makes taxation feel like theft.

But equating taxation and theft is difficult to defend. A country without taxes couldn't field an army, after all, and would soon be overrun by a country that had one. Its residents would then have to pay taxes to that country. A country without mandatory taxation is the political analog of a highly unstable isotope in chemistry.

The philosophers Liam Murphy and Thomas Nagel have argued that there has never been any presumption that citizens are morally entitled to keep their entire pre-tax incomes.[10] Governments provide services that citizens value, and those services must be paid for. Elected legislators in any democracy vote on what the tax rates should be, and citizens are then entitled to keep only their post-tax incomes. It goes without saying that few people actually enjoy paying taxes. Yet a world without taxes would be demonstrably worse.

Growing government budget deficits around the globe have resulted in no small part from insistent demands from top earners for tax cuts. Some have advocated such cuts as part of a "starve-the-beast strategy," in which depriving the government of revenue would supposedly help eliminate government waste. But government programs exist because important constituents want them and are therefore extremely difficult to cut. Cuts, when they do come, typically occur not where they would make the most sense, but where those who would suffer from them are least able to push back. An important result of deficits has thus been to reduce our investment in the future. The unborn citizens who will suffer as a result are simply unable to protest.

With tens of millions of baby boomers slated to enter retirement during the coming years, fiscal experts warn that we will not be able to balance our budgets and make essential investments going forward without substantial new revenue. And since most of the income gains during the past four decades have accrued to those atop the earnings ladder, most of that revenue would have to come from the wealthy. As Willie Sutton was said to have responded when asked why he robbed banks, "That's where the money is."

We may assume that those who are more keenly aware of the importance of luck in their lives are also more likely to feel grateful for any successes they've enjoyed. How might such feelings affect their willingness to help maintain the infrastructure that helped them succeed? The Northeastern University psychologist David DeSteno has conducted a variety of experiments on gratitude that help to answer this question.

In one widely cited study, for example, he and his coauthors devised a clever manipulation to make a group of laboratory subjects feel grateful, and then gave them an opportunity to take actions that would benefit others at their own expense.[11] Subjects were divided into a treatment group (those in whom feelings of gratitude were induced) and a control group (in which no attempt was made to induce such feelings). Both groups were first seated in front of individual computer terminals and asked to record whether letters flashed on the screen before them constituted English words. The task was designed to be tedious, and subjects were asked to perform it as quickly as possible before moving to the next phase of the experiment.

When those in the treatment group had completed their task and were awaiting feedback on their performance, their computers appeared to crash. At that moment, a confederate of the researchers who was seated at an adjacent computer terminal asked whether she could help, explaining that she'd managed to revive one of the lab's computers after it had crashed during her participation in an earlier experiment.

In each case, the distressed subject accepted the offer of assistance. After executing a series of keystrokes, the confederate "fixed" the computer, which rebooted with the subject's results from the earlier task intact. Exit questionnaires later confirmed that this manipulation caused subjects in the treatment group to report feelings of gratitude for the help they thought they'd received. A control group of subjects went through exactly the same sequence but did not experience a computer crash. In those cases, a confederate spoke briefly with the subject about a neutral topic before both proceeded to the next stage of the experiment.

Subjects from both the treatment and control groups were then asked to play an economic game that probed their willingness to take costly action for the common good. They were assigned partners, and both were initially given four tokens that could be redeemed for $1 each if they kept them, but that would be worth $2 each if transferred to their partners. The best outcome for a pair of players would thus be for each to give all four tokens to the partner, in which case each would receive a payoff of $8. But players were not allowed to discuss their decision beforehand, so transferring all their tokens was a risky move, since there was no guarantee that their partners would do the same. Purely selfish players, then, would be tempted to keep all four tokens, thereby earning at least $4 (compared to the $0 they would get if they transferred four tokens and their partner transferred none), and as much as $12 (if their partners transferred all four tokens).

The number of tokens a player chooses to transfer is thus a useful measure of the player's public spiritedness. Each pair of partners played the game only once, thereby eliminating the possibility of retaliation in future rounds. Players were told that their partners were stationed at computers in a different room, and half of the subjects from both the treatment and control groups were told that they were paired with the person they had

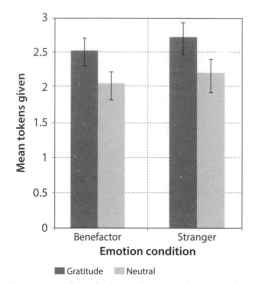

FIGURE 6.2. Average number of tokens given as a function of emotion condition and game partner. "Benefactor" refers to known partners (who provided help to subjects in the treatment group but not to those in the control group). Source: David DeSteno et al., "Gratitude as Moral Sentiment: Emotion-Guided Cooperation in Economic Exchange," *Emotion* 10.2 (2010): 289–93.

spoken with during the earlier stage of the experiment (the confederate). The remaining subjects were told that their partner was a stranger.

The results of this experiment are summarized in figure 6.2, in which the dark rectangles measure the average number of tokens transferred by subjects in the treatment group and the light rectangles measure the corresponding averages for subjects in the control group. Note that subjects in the treatment group—those in whom the emotion of gratitude had been induced—transferred an average of at least 25 percent more to their partners than did subjects in the control group. As DeSteno and his coauthors emphasize, the greater generosity of the grateful subjects cannot be attributed to norms of reciprocity, since they were actually slightly more generous in their transfers to perfect strangers than they were to the confederates they believed had helped them.

In an earlier study that employed a similar gratitude induction, DeSteno and Monica Bartlett examined the willingness of subjects to respond to requests for assistance—in some cases from the confederate who had helped them in an earlier stage of the experiment and in other cases from strangers.[12] As shown in figure 6.3, subjects in whom gratitude had been induced spent more time assisting those who had asked for help than did subjects in the neutral condition.

These findings suggest that if people who acknowledge luck's role in their lives are indeed more likely than others to feel

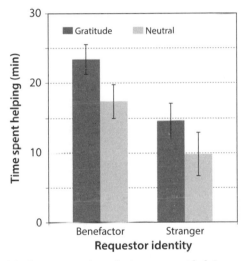

FIGURE 6.3. Average number of minutes spent helping as a function of emotion condition and game partner. "Benefactor" refers to known partners (who provided help to subjects in the treatment group but not to those in the control group).
Source: Monica Bartlett and David DeSteno, "Gratitude and Prosocial Behavior: Helping When It Costs You," *Psychological Science* 17.4 (April 2006): 319–25.

grateful for any success they've enjoyed, they're also more likely to share some of the fruits of their efforts to support the common good.

In her memoir about her father, Charles Dickens's daughter Mamie recalls a Christmas gathering in which he advised his assembled children to "Reflect on your present blessings, of which every man has many, not on your past misfortunes, of which all men have some."[13] Recent work in psychology suggests that heeding that advice may make people not only more willing to contribute to the common good but also more likely to experience happiness and good health.

In one study, for example, the psychologists Robert Emmons and Michael McCullough asked a group of people to keep diaries in which they noted things that had happened each week that had made them feel grateful, a second group to note things that had made them feel irritated, and a third simply to record things that had affected them.[14] Ten weeks into the process, those who had written about gratitude were significantly more optimistic than participants in the other two groups, and also reported elevated levels of subjective well-being (the psychologists' term for happiness). Participants in the gratitude group also appeared to enjoy better health than the others, as measured by their having exercised more and made fewer visits to physicians.

In another study, the psychologist Martin Seligman and his coauthors asked people to engage in five exercises that had been shown in earlier work to boost feelings of well-being.[15] One was to write and personally deliver a letter of gratitude to someone who had never been properly thanked for an earlier kindness. This step, they found, was associated with a larger and more persistent increase in happiness scores than any other of the four other exercises.

Numerous other studies by psychologists report similar findings. Nancy Digdon and Amy Koble found that experimental subjects who were induced to feel gratitude toward others experienced subsequent reductions in anxiety and sounder sleep patterns.[16] Nathan DeWall and his collaborators showed that people in whom feelings of gratitude had been induced were also more likely to experience empathy toward others and less likely to respond aggressively when provoked by others.[17]

♠

Failure to appreciate luck's importance is of course not the only reason the wealthy have been lobbying for additional tax cuts. But it's an important reason. The problem is compounded by the fact that disdain for luck is often greatest in those who possess the most power to influence political decisions about the tax code.

Consider Stephen Schwarzman, the CEO of Blackstone, the fabled private-equity firm. Schwarzman lives well. He made the news in 2007 when he staged a $3-million sixtieth birthday party for himself and several hundred of his closest friends at the Armory on Park Avenue. According to *Gawker's* coverage of the event, "Rod Stewart was paid $1 million to perform for the assembled guests; Patti LaBelle sang 'Happy Birthday.' And the room was designed to replicate Schwarzman's $40 million co-op at 740 Park Avenue."[18] But Schwarzman believes the government is taking far too much of "his" money.

James Surowiecki, an economics writer for the *New Yorker*, offered these thoughts on the Blackstone executive:

> The past few years have been very good to Stephen Schwarzman.... His industry, which relies on borrowed money, has benefitted from low interest rates, and the stock-market boom has given his firm great opportunities to cash out investments. Schwarzman is now worth more

than ten billion dollars. You wouldn't think he'd have much to complain about. But, to hear him tell it, he's beset by a meddlesome, tax-happy government and a whiny, envious populace. He recently grumbled that the U.S. middle class has taken to "blaming wealthy people" for its problems. Previously, he has said that it might be good to raise income taxes on the poor so they had "skin in the game," and that proposals to repeal the carried-interest tax loophole—from which he personally benefits—were akin to the German invasion of Poland.[19]

Surowiecki went on to note that other wealthy executives have been voicing similar complaints. The venture capitalist Tom Perkins and the Home Depot cofounder Kenneth Langone, for example, each recently likened populist criticism of the wealthy to the Nazis' attacks on the Jews.

Schwarzman and others have also been channeling vast sums to political action committees that lobby for still lower top tax rates and even less strict business regulation. And their political power to achieve these aims has increased significantly in the wake of recent campaign finance rulings by the Supreme Court.

The result has been a systemic positive feedback loop of the sort that explains many instances of market success at the individual level. People succeed on a spectacular scale, then use some of their gains to win more favorable tax and regulatory treatment, which increases their wealth still further, enabling them to buy even more favorable treatment, and so on.

Because processes like these gather steam over time, it's easy for those who favor change to lose hope. But just as hopelessness makes it more difficult to surmount obstacles along individual paths to success, it also inhibits social change. So it's important for advocates of change not to lose hope, provided any reasonable grounds for hope remain.

As President Nixon's chief economist Herb Stein once famously remarked, "If something cannot go on forever, it will stop."[20] But what, exactly, could stop a process that grows steadily more powerful over time? The answer is an opposing process that also grows steadily more powerful over time. Those lobbying for lower taxes and less stringent regulation are unlikely to change their behavior in response to appeals on behalf of society as a whole. Most of them no doubt sincerely believe that their own interests coincide with society's. Yet compelling evidence suggests that our current patterns of private and public spending have been deeply counterproductive, not just for poor and middle-income families, but also for the wealthy themselves. If the wealthy were exposed to this evidence, they might find it convincing. Fundamental policy change would surely become a much easier sell if more wealthy people realized how poorly current arrangements serve their interests.

An experience some years ago persuaded me that even small shifts in cognitive framing can dramatically transform how people think about such things. During a sabbatical year my family and I spent in Paris, our youngest son, Hayden, came home from school one afternoon in a state of high agitation. He'd been given an *avertissement*—or disciplinary notice—for something he hadn't done. A playground supervisor had complained that a student had shouted an obscenity at him, but since the supervisor couldn't identify the specific offender, he'd simply filed charges against every student playing nearby, a group that included Hayden.

Insisting that he'd done nothing wrong, Hayden thought we should demand a hearing. But when I made a few inquiries, I learned that receiving a single avertissement from the school had absolutely no consequences. A notice mattered only for students who had already received three previous ones during the same school year.

I then told Hayden that the French system simply handled things differently from what we were used to at home. I reminded him that even a detailed investigation of the episode wouldn't guarantee that the authorities would get all the facts right. He seemed to accept that the French system would settle things justly most of the time, since students who got four disciplinary notices in a single year had probably done *something* wrong. Applying that new cognitive frame to the problem completely defused his moral outrage.

In similar fashion, I've seen even brief discussions of the link between success and luck temper the outrage many wealthy people feel about taxes. At an intuitive level, it's not puzzling that successful citizens like Schwarzman might view mandatory taxation as unjustified confiscation of what's rightfully theirs. But that's an unfruitful way to think about taxes. Extensive public investment was an essential precondition for the economic prosperity of those very same tax protesters, and we can't have public investment without taxes.

Sensible views about taxes or any other subject do not reliably triumph over less sensible ones in the short run. But we should all take comfort in the fact that the long-run historical narrative bends toward truth. One reason is that when evidence for a particular view becomes compelling, the number of people who embrace it tends to snowball. Beliefs are contagious.

One of the clearest recent illustrations has been the evolution of opinion regarding the permissibility of same-sex marriage in the United States. Not even a decade ago, substantial majorities in all parts of the country were vehemently opposed to it. Yet by 2010 opinion had become evenly divided, and by the spring of 2014, 59 percent of Americans endorsed marriage equality while only 34 percent were opposed.[21]

The conversations driving this shift were stimulated in part by media coverage of specific individuals involved in same-sex

Elmer Lokkins (*left*) and Gustavo Archilla.
Photo: James Estrin/The New York Times/Redux.

relationships. Elmer Lokkins and Gustavo Archilla, who met in New York City in 1945 and lived quietly together for fifty-eight years, had kept the nature of their relationship private even from close relatives. Then in 2003, shortly after Canada legalized same-sex marriage, the two traveled north to make their bond official. "Canada made it possible for us," Mr. Archilla told a crowd of well-wishers at New York City's annual Wedding March in 2007. "I hope everywhere else it will soon be possible. Maybe, while we are still alive, though there is not much time left."[22]

Not even the most outspoken advocates of marriage equality foresaw how rapidly opinion would shift on this issue. Nor, for that matter, did pundits predict the sudden collapse of the former Soviet Union, or the events of the Arab Spring. In each case, volatility and unpredictability were simply inherent features of social belief systems.[23]

Public opinion shifts one conversation at a time. In my own recent conversations with highly successful people, I've seen opinions change on the spot. Many who seem never to have considered the possibility that their success stemmed from factors other than their own talent and effort are often surprisingly willing to rethink. In many instances, even brief reflection stimulates them to recall specific examples of good breaks they've enjoyed along the way.

Tax resistance spawned by failure to appreciate luck's pivotal role in success has made it harder to sustain the public investment needed to support the stock of luck available to future generations. But, as we'll presently see, it has also resulted in spending patterns that poorly serve the current generation, including even its most successful members.

7
♠

WE'RE IN LUCK:

A GOLDEN OPPORTUNITY

Becoming better at playing the piano requires many hours of practice, time that's no longer available for other things. Staying up a little longer with a detective novel on Sunday night means getting by with a little less sleep on Monday. Spending $2,000 on a new bike means having $2,000 less to spend on travel and entertainment. As economists like to say, there's no free lunch. By this we mean simply that all things we value come at a cost, explicit or implicit.

But there's an apparent exception to this principle. Suppose, for example, that you and others were each about to spend $2,000 on something that, once you had it, would prove worthless to you. By not making that purchase, you could buy the $2,000 bike you wanted without giving anything up. I call this an apparent exception to the no-free-lunch principle, because even here, buying the bike would mean not being able to spend that $2,000 on other things. The fact remains, however, that if there were an expensive new thing you wanted, it would be a lot easier to get it if you had wasteful expenditures you could eliminate.

Most of us are already pretty careful about how we spend our money, of course, so it might seem difficult to find waste to eliminate. As we'll see, however, our spending patterns actually entail waste on a grand scale, easily amounting to several trillion dollars a year in the aggregate. This waste occurs not because we spend carelessly, but rather because our individual spending incentives are often squarely at odds with our collective interests. Imagine a sports arena where all the fans stand to get a better view, only to discover that no one sees any better than if they all had remained comfortably seated. Our individual incentives lead us to spend money in ways that are mutually offsetting in analogous ways.

How much, for example, do parents feel they need to spend on their daughter's wedding? They want guests to remember it as a special occasion, but "special" is a relative concept. Fast food hamburgers for the reception dinner would of course be ill-advised in most cases. But how much should they spend on catering and floral arrangements?

Standards differ from place to place and from era to era. In 1980, the cost of an average American wedding, adjusted for inflation, was $11,000, a princely sum in most parts of the world even today. But by 2014, that figure had escalated to $30,000, and in Manhattan the average wedding now costs more than $76,000.[1]

Why are people spending so much more? The short answer is that the standards that define "special" have escalated sharply. I'll say more about why that's happened, but for now note that today's more expensive weddings have not made marrying couples any happier. On the contrary, it appears that increased expenditures on weddings may actually make them more likely to divorce.[2] If an across-the-board rollback in wedding expenditures would leave wedding celebrants no less happy than before, then this particular escalation in expenditures qualifies as pure waste.

What's more, there are simple, unintrusive policy measures that could free up a large share of the resources currently being wasted in similar ways—more than enough to address even our most difficult environmental and economic problems. We could make the educational investments that help foster success, tackle our infrastructure maintenance backlog, expand health care coverage, ameliorate climate change, and do much to reduce poverty, all without requiring painful sacrifices from anyone.

If that claim strikes you as far-fetched, you'll be surprised to see that it rests on only five simple premises, none of them controversial.

1. FRAMES OF REFERENCE MATTER. A LOT.

Which of the two horizontal lines below is longer?

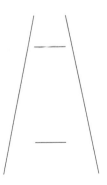

If you suspect a trick, you may say they're the same, and indeed they are. But if you really think they LOOK the same, you should schedule a neurological checkup. To the normal human brain, the line on top looks longer, simply because of where it sits.

Economists have been slow to recognize that similar framing effects shape our evaluations of almost every good we buy. Earlier I mentioned my two-room house in Nepal with no electricity or plumbing. If I lived in that same house in the United States, my children would have been ashamed to invite friends over. Yet in Nepal it was a completely satisfactory house.

If my Nepalese friends could see my house in Ithaca, New York, they'd think I'd taken leave of my senses. They'd wonder why anyone would need such a grand home. Why so many bathrooms? But most Americans don't think that. That's because our evaluations depend so heavily on what's nearby.

2. EACH PERSON'S SPENDING DEPENDS IN PART ON WHAT OTHERS SPEND.

Standard economic models assume that each person's spending is completely independent of what others spend. But if framing effects matter, that can't be right.

People spend more when their friends and neighbors spend more. This isn't some fantastic new discovery. It's a dynamic we've known about since the dawn of time. Many have called it "keeping up with the Joneses." But I've never liked that expression, because it summons images of insecure people trying to appear wealthier than they are. Peer influences would in fact be just as strong in a world completely free of jealousy and envy.

Rising inequality has made framing effects stronger. The median new house in the United States is now 50 percent larger than it was in 1980, even though the median income has grown only slightly in real terms. The fact that houses are growing faster than incomes for middle-income families is difficult to explain without invoking a process I call expenditure cascades.

Here's how it works. People at the top begin building bigger houses simply because they have more money. Perhaps it's become the custom for them to have their daughters' wedding receptions at home, so a ballroom is now part of what defines an adequate living space. Those houses shift the frame of reference for the near-wealthy—who travel in the same social circles—so they, too, build bigger. But as the near-wealthy begin adding Sub-Zero refrigerators and vaulted ceilings, they shift the frames of reference that define adequate for upper-middle class families. And so those families start saving less and borrowing more to keep pace. And so it goes, all the way down the income ladder. More spending by the people at the top ultimately creates pressure for more spending by people at the bottom, for whom the additional outlays are often a difficult stretch.

3. THE COSTS OF FAILURE TO KEEP PACE WITH COMMUNITY
SPENDING NORMS GO WELL BEYOND MERE HURT FEELINGS.

Why don't people simply summon more self-discipline and opt out of the rat race? After all, Congress isn't mandating that people buy bigger houses than they can afford. One reason is that opting out entails real costs that are extremely hard to avoid.

Failure to keep pace with what peers spend on housing means not just living in a house that seems uncomfortably small. It means also having to send your children to inferior schools. A "good" school is a relative concept, and the better schools are almost always those in more expensive neighborhoods. To send their children to a school of at least average quality, median earners must buy the median-priced home in their area. An indirect consequence of the higher housing expenditures by top earners is that median home prices have also risen sharply.

I came up with a simple measure I call the "toil index" (see figure 7.1), which tracks the monthly number of hours the median earner must work to rent a house in the median school

Hours per month

Monthly hours of work required for
median worker to earn median rent

FIGURE 7.1. The toil index.

district. When incomes were growing at the same rate for everyone during the early post-WWII decades, the index was almost
completely stable. But income inequality began rising sharply
after 1970, and since then the toil index has been rising in tandem. For the past ten years, it's been approximately one hundred hours a month, up from only forty-two hours in 1970.

The median real hourly wage for men in the United States
is actually lower now than in the 1980s. If middle-income families must now spend more than before to achieve basic goals,
how do they manage? Census data reveal clear symptoms of
increasing financial distress among these families. Of the one
hundred largest US counties, those where income inequality
grew most rapidly were also those that experienced the largest
increases in three important symptoms of financial distress:
divorce rates, long commutes, and bankruptcy filings.[3] In de-

veloped countries tracked by the Organization for Economic Cooperation and Development, higher inequality is associated with longer work hours, both across countries and over time.[4] Standard economic models predict none of these relationships.

Expenditure cascades have also occurred in other areas, such as celebrations to mark special occasions. Without reference to this process, it's very difficult to explain the sharp escalation in wedding costs discussed earlier. The multimillion-dollar coming-of-age parties staged by the wealthiest families have similarly raised the standards that govern spending on such events by families further down the income ladder. Many middle-income children are now disappointed when birthday parties fail to feature a professional clown or magician.

Concerns about relative position are a hard fact of human nature. No biologist is surprised that they loom so large in human psychology, since relative position was always by far the best predictor of reproductive success. People who didn't care how well they were doing in relative terms would have been ill-equipped for the competitive environments in which we evolved. Few parents, on reflection, would want their children to be stripped of positional concerns completely.

But even though positional concerns are an essential component of human psychology, not all their consequences are benign.

4. POSITIONAL CONCERNS SPAWN WASTEFUL SPENDING, EVEN WHEN EVERYONE IS WELL INFORMED AND RATIONAL.

Charles Darwin, the great British naturalist, was heavily influenced by Adam Smith and other economists. He saw that competition in nature, like competition in the marketplace, often produced benefits for both individuals and larger groups, just as in Smith's Invisible Hand theory. Keen eyesight in hawks,

Large antlers: good for individual bulls, bad for bulls as a group.
Photo: Duke Coonrad.

for example, made both individual hawks and hawks as a species more successful. Yet Darwin also saw that many traits and behaviors helped individuals at the expense of larger groups. When success depends on relative position, as it almost always does in competitive struggles, wasteful "positional arms races" often result.

Consider the antlers in bull elk, which can span four feet and weigh as much as forty pounds. Because those unwieldy appendages impair mobility in wooded areas, they put bulls at greater risk of being surrounded and killed by wolves. So why doesn't natural selection favor smaller antlers? Darwin's answer was that large antlers evolved because elk are a polygynous species, meaning that males take more than one mate if they can. But if some take multiple mates, others are left with none. That's why males fight so bitterly with one another for access to females. Mutations that coded for larger antlers spread quickly because any bull that had them was more likely to win. A bull with smaller antlers would be less vulnerable to predators, but he would also be less likely to pass his genes on to the next generation.

Bulls would be better off as a group if each animal's antlers were smaller by half. Each fight would be decided in the same way as before, while the elk would all be less vulnerable to predators. The inefficiency in such positional arms races is analogous to the inefficiency in military arms races.

This important point is not understood as clearly as it should be. In a 2011 book, I described the close parallels between military arms races and the evolutionary forces that spawned outsized antlers in bull elk.[5] Shortly after the book was published, science writer John Whitfield's review of it appeared in *Slate* under the inauspicious title, "Libertarians with Antlers: What Robert H. Frank's *The Darwin Economy* Gets Wrong about Evolution."[6] Whitfield objected that if big antlers were harmful, natural selection would have long since solved that problem by weeding out any bulls whose antlers were too large. But that objection ignores the logic that explains why arms races are wasteful in the first place.

The race to stockpile military armaments doesn't go on without limit, since citizens of a nation that spent all its income on weapons would starve. By the same token, the race to achieve large relative antler size doesn't go on without limit. We don't see bulls with antlers spanning forty feet and weighing four hundred pounds, since such animals would never be able to lift their noses from the turf, much less compete successfully for mates. But the fact that these arms races are self-limiting doesn't mean that the stocks of bombs aren't wasteful, or that four-foot antlers are an attractive option for bulls collectively. If bulls could somehow agree to scale back all antler racks by half, they'd clearly be better off.[7]

This simple point applies not just to antler size but also to the amounts people spend on things whose value is highly context-sensitive. Beyond some point, additional spending on mansions, coming-of-age parties, and many other goods becomes purely positional, meaning that it merely raises the bar that defines adequate. Because much of the total spending in today's economy is purely positional, it is wasteful in the same way that military arms races are wasteful.

Although positional concerns spawn trillions of dollars of unproductive spending each year, we're in luck.

5. THE GOOD NEWS IS THAT A SIMPLE CHANGE IN THE TAX SYSTEM WOULD ELIMINATE MANY WASTEFUL SPENDING PATTERNS.

Elk lack the cognitive and communication skills to do anything about their particular positional arms race. But humans can and do enact positional arms control agreements. We spend too much on houses and parties because as individuals we have no incentive to take account of how our spending affects others. But the tax system offers a simple, unintrusive way to change our incentives. We could abandon the current progressive income tax in favor of a much more steeply progressive consumption tax.

Here's how it would work: People would report their incomes as they do now, and also their annual savings, as many already do for tax-exempt retirement accounts. Their income minus their savings is their annual consumption, and that amount less a large standard deduction would be their taxable consumption. For instance, a family that earned $100,000 and saved $20,000 in a tax year would have an annual consumption of $80,000. If the standard deduction were $30,000, this family's taxable consumption would be $50,000.

The tax rate would start out low and would then rise steadily as taxable consumption increased. Under the current income tax, rates can't rise too high without choking off savings and investment. But higher marginal tax rates on consumption would actually encourage savings and investment.

Many wealthy people think higher taxes would make them less able to get what they want. But as discussed earlier, what happens when everyone spends less is very different from what happens when an individual spends less. In a society with a progressive consumption tax, the wealthiest drivers might buy a Porsche 911 Turbo for $150,000 rather than a Ferrari Berlinetta F12 for more than twice that amount. But since everyone would be scaling back, that society's Porsche owners would be just as excited about their cars as Ferrari owners are under the current tax system.

There's another important dimension to the argument: A progressive consumption tax would generate additional revenue that could help pay for better infrastructure. Under the current tax structure, the rich can afford their Ferraris but must drive them on poorly maintained roads. And the experience of a Ferrari driver on roads riddled with potholes is significantly less satisfying than that of a Porsche driver on well-maintained roads.

My basic claim is that, without demanding painful sacrifices from anyone, this relatively simple policy change would enable us to put trillions of dollars a year to work rebuilding the institutions and infrastructure that reliably translate talent and effort into success—in other words, the kind of environment people would be lucky to be born into. This claim will strike many people as fanciful. Yet the argument in favor of it has few moving parts, and none of the premises on which it rests is controversial.

Most income gains have been going to top earners, which has led them to build bigger houses. Evidence shows that, beyond some point, across-the-board increases in mansion size don't make the rich any happier. Yet these larger houses at the top have shifted the frame of reference that shapes the demands of those just below them, and so on, all the way down the income ladder. The resulting financial squeeze on middle-income families has not only made it more difficult for those families to pay their bills; it has also made it more difficult for governments to raise revenue. And that, in turn, has led to a decline in the quality of infrastructure and public services.

Despite their higher incomes, then, the rich now appear to be worse off on balance. Their higher spending on cars and houses has simply raised the bar that defines adequate in those categories, while the corresponding decline in the quality of public goods has had a significant negative impact. But because the profoundly wasteful spending patterns that result from these framing effects could be changed by a simple revision in the tax code, we're in luck.

Some have objected that many people are now so wealthy that they would simply ignore a progressive consumption tax in their spending decisions. But that objection is at odds with how even the wealthiest people respond to higher prices. In New York City, which has some of the highest prices per square foot of real estate anywhere in the world, even multibillionaires rarely live in apartments larger than 8,000 square feet. Most of these people will eventually die with enough assets to have bought the entire building that houses their apartments. Yet they choose not to, perhaps because New York's high prices have made it socially acceptable for even the hyper-rich to live in more modest spaces. But if those same multibillionaires lived, say, in Dallas, they'd think nothing of buying 20,000-square-foot mansions.

We should thus expect a progressive consumption tax to encourage many wealthy people to rethink their plans for $2-million mansion additions. Since the after-tax price of such projects would be much higher than before, many would scale back, perhaps instructing their architects to show them what $1-million additions might look like instead.

If they and others decided to go with smaller projects, they might expect the results to be disappointing relative to the larger additions they'd originally planned. But as we've seen, what happens when everyone spends less is very different from what happens when any single individual spends less. So if all scale back in tandem, the smaller additions will serve just as well as the larger ones would have. More important, a progressive consumption tax would also generate additional revenue that could help pay for better public goods and services.

Therein lies the fiscal alchemy inherent in the progressive consumption tax. By inhibiting a collection of largely unproductive expenditure cascades, it would effectively create new resources out of thin air.

Some worry that a progressive consumption tax would undercut people's incentives to work hard and invest in the future. But Darwin's insight that life is graded on the curve suggests otherwise. No change in rules or tax policy could ever extinguish the human impulse to get ahead. But getting ahead is an almost purely relative concept. It means doing better than one's rivals, and a progressive consumption tax wouldn't alter the fact that those who earn more can also spend more.

Others have worried that a progressive consumption tax would make life more difficult for those who take special pleasure in material possessions. But this tax would not in any way diminish the supply of nice things to be had. There are only so many penthouse apartments in New York City with sweeping views of Central Park, and although a progressive consumption tax would reduce what people could bid for those apartments, it would not change the identities of the winning bidders.

A progressive consumption tax would, however, reduce the share of national income consumed while increasing the share invested. The growth sparked by that greater investment would increase future incomes. And that means that future consumption levels, though smaller as a share of national income, would eventually be higher in absolute terms than they would have been under current arrangements. So even those who believe that satisfaction depends more on absolute consumption than on relative consumption have no reason to fear a progressive consumption tax.

Some have objected to the progressive consumption tax on the grounds that it legitimizes base emotions like jealousy and envy, which they feel merit no consideration in the design of public policy. The libertarian economist Donald Boudreaux, for example, has said,

> I agree that people are concerned about their relative standing in society. But I don't believe that such a concern should necessarily be embodied in government policy. (I also agree with those who point out that people naturally are biased against foreigners—prejudiced against others whose appearance and language and customs are very different from what is familiar but I don't want to elevate this natural tribal impulse into government policy.)

Boudreaux and others reject policies based on positional concerns for the same reason they would oppose giving policy weight to the preferences of sadists.

We do indeed have legitimate reasons for discouraging our children from envying the good fortune of others. But positional concerns stem much less from envy than from the simple fact that many important rewards in life depend on relative position. Only a small proportion of home sites have sweeping views, and who gets them is best predicted by relative income.

Perhaps even more important, context is the very wellspring of the everyday quality judgments that drive consumer demand. That the significance of this point is not widely appreciated first became clear to me during a conversation that took place the evening before a lecture I gave some years ago. Two of my faculty hosts and I were waiting outside a restaurant when the fourth member of our party pulled up behind the wheel of a brand new Lexus sedan. Once we were seated at our table, the Lexus owner's first words to me, unbidden, were that he didn't know or care what kinds of cars his neighbors and colleagues drove. As it happened, I had had numerous conversations with this gentleman over the years and found his statement completely credible.

I asked him why he had chosen the Lexus over the much cheaper, but equally reliable, Toyota sedan from the same manufacturer. He responded that it was the car's quality that had attracted him—things like the look and feel of its interior materials, the sound its doors made on closing, and so on. He mentioned with special pride that the car's engine was so quiet and vibration-free that the owner's manual posted warnings in red letters against attempting to start the car while its engine was already running.

His previous car, he told us, had none of these attractive features. I then asked him how he thought people would have reacted to that car if it had been possible to transport it back to the year 1935 in a time capsule. He answered without hesitation that anyone from that era would have been extremely impressed. They would have found the car's acceleration and handling spectacular; its interior materials would have amazed them; and its engine would have seemed unbelievably quiet.

We then discussed what a formal mathematical model of the demand for automobile quality might look like, agreeing that any reasonable one would incorporate a comparison of the car's features with the corresponding features of other cars in the same local environment. Cars that scored positively in such comparisons would be seen as having high quality, for which consumers would be willing to pay a premium. I then pointed out that this model would be essentially identical to one based on a desire, not to own quality for its own sake, but rather to outdo, or avoid being outdone by, one's friends and neighbors.

Yet the subjective impressions conveyed by these two descriptions could hardly be more different. To demand quality for its own sake is to be a discerning buyer. But to wish to outdo one's friends and neighbors is to be a jackass.

I noticed that on the heels of this discussion, everyone at the table suddenly took much more interest in talking about the kinds of behavior that are driven by contextual concerns. It was fine to talk about behaviors that result from context-dependent perceptions of quality, but not at all palatable to speak of behaviors that result from envy or a desire to outdo others.

In short, we can embrace the progressive consumption tax without voicing approval of emotions like envy or jealousy. This tax is attractive on purely practical grounds.

If we continue on our current course, additional growth in income inequality will produce future expenditure cascades that will dwarf the ones we've witnessed so far. Houses will continue to grow larger and wedding costs will continue to rise, causing families to feel pressure to spend money that could be much better devoted to other things.

But although I've been writing about the attractions of the progressive consumption tax for decades, we seem no closer to adopting one. Indeed, there's essentially no chance that Congress would even discuss, much less adopt, a progressive consumption tax this year. But even if Congress astonished everyone by endorsing one today, it would probably be better not to implement it right away.

That's because lingering effects of the Great Recession have held total spending below the level necessary to support employment for all who want to work. In an ideal world, we'd respond to that shortfall by aggressively tackling our backlog of overdue infrastructure maintenance. But absent additional spending of that sort, encouraging even wasteful consumption spending would be better than doing nothing. The mere announcement that a progressive consumption tax was coming would stimulate hundreds of billions of dollars of additional private spending. Building larger mansions may not make the wealthy any happier, but it does create jobs for unemployed architects and carpenters.

Phased in gradually when the economy is back at full employment, a progressive consumption tax would induce a gradual shift in the composition of national spending. The proportion devoted to luxury consumption would slowly decline, while the proportion devoted to investment would slowly rise. A progressive consumption tax implemented in that way would not reduce the number of jobs; it would merely alter the mix of tasks that get done.

If the progressive consumption tax is such a good idea, why haven't we already adopted it? In one sense, we have, since more than 90 percent of Americans are currently below the upper limits on tax-deferred savings permitted in supplemental retirement savings accounts. For those households, current spending incentives are essentially the same as they would be under a progressive consumption tax. But households with the highest incomes save much more than the ceilings on supplemental retirement accounts. And since it's the spending of those households that launch the expenditure cascades just described, our current system does nothing to encourage restraint on their part. So the question remains: Why haven't we already adopted a full-blown progressive consumption tax?

It's a question I've discussed with many people. Cornell University often sends me to speak to alumni groups around the country, and on many of those occasions I've described why abandoning the progressive income tax in favor of a progressive consumption tax would produce a better outcome for almost everyone. The responses I've received from these groups, most of which are heavily composed of National Public Radio listeners, share a common theme: The proposal sounds like a good idea, but there's essentially no chance of persuading conservatives to go along with it.

But that's an overly pessimistic assessment. Occasionally, for example, I speak to an alumni group in a deep red enclave, and many of the staunchest conservatives in those audiences are also quick to embrace the progressive consumption tax once they've heard the case for it. (It's of course easier to make that case in alumni forums than in the political arena, where thirty-second sound bites are the dominant mode of communication.)

I'll note, too, that a week after an article I'd written about the progressive consumption tax was published in 1997,[8] I received a thick envelope in the mail bearing the return address of Professor Milton Friedman, the patron saint of small-government conservatism. His letter began by saying that he'd enjoyed my article but didn't share my view that the government should be raising and spending more money. With government budgets then inching toward surplus during President Clinton's second term, that was hardly surprising. But Friedman went on to say that if the government did need additional revenue, the progressive consumption tax would be by far the most effective way to raise it. The envelope was thick because he'd enclosed a copy of his own article, published in the *American Economic Review* in 1943, in which he'd argued that the progressive consumption tax would be the best way to finance the war effort.[9]

Additional evidence of the progressive consumption tax's ability to attract bipartisan support surfaced when Senators Pete Domenici (R, NM) and Sam Nunn (D, GA) proposed what they called the Unlimited Savings Allowance Tax in 1995.[10] Their USA tax was essentially identical to the tax I'm proposing.

Other budget battles kept their proposal from coming up for a vote, but no one at the time characterized it as a radical idea.

Although we see widespread hostility to new taxes of any kind today, two senior scholars at the American Enterprise Institute, a conservative think tank in Washington, DC, published a 2012 book extolling the virtues of the progressive consumption tax.[11] The authors, economists Alan Viard and Robert Carroll, make no mention of its potential to curtail expenditure cascades. They like the tax because they believe, correctly, that it will stimulate much needed savings and investment. But it's an even better policy instrument than they think.

In short, it seems premature to write off the progressive consumption tax as a political nonstarter.

Congress probably won't seriously consider a progressive consumption tax in the absence of a dire fiscal crisis. But with tens of millions of baby boomer retirements looming, such a crisis is only a matter of time. At some point in the not-too-distant future, then, we'll be forced to recognize the need for additional revenue. And at that point the progressive consumption tax will be on the table.

If it's enacted and people have an opportunity to experience its effects for a few years, they will appreciate how lucky we were that our historical spending patterns were so wasteful. Without having to make any painful sacrifices, we will have been able to make long overdue investments that greatly benefit everyone.

It's a golden opportunity that's ours for the taking.

8
♠

BEING GRATEFUL

In his 1983 novel *Mr. Palomar*, Italo Calvino describes his title character's thoughts during a stroll on a Mediterranean beach. When Palomar realizes he is approaching a topless sunbather, he quickly directs his gaze seaward, wanting to respect the woman's privacy. But once he has passed, it occurs to him that in looking away he has unwittingly endorsed the belief, which he finds distasteful, that the sight of the human breast is somehow illicit.

On his return walk, he therefore adopts a different posture. As he approaches the woman a second time, he keeps his eyes fixed straight ahead, attempting to convey an attitude of complete neutrality, his gaze counting for no more than that of a seagull. But that can't be right, either, he decides moments later. Now he worries that he has reduced the breast to a mere object.

So Palomar turns back and again walks toward the woman, this time hoping to convey an attitude of neutral objectivity. But once past her, he worries that the woman might have misinterpreted the grazing of his eyes as a sense of superiority. Still determined to get it right, he reverses course yet again. "Now his gaze, giving the landscape a fickle glance, will linger on the breast with special consideration, but will quickly include in it an impulse of good will and gratitude for the whole, for the sun and the sky, for the bent pines and the dune and the beach and the rocks and the clouds and the seaweed, for the cosmos that rotates around those hallowed cusps."[1]

And this time the woman springs up, covers herself, and leaves in a huff. Palomar ruefully concludes that the "dead weight of an intolerant tradition prevents anyone's properly understanding the most enlightened intentions."[2]

Mr. Palomar is not alone in his concern about the opinions of others. People who enjoy the admiration and affection of their peers are not just happier because of that fact; they're also more likely to prosper. That's in part because most of the biggest economic success stories are team efforts. Almost everyone wants to enjoy the benefits of collaborating with talented teammates. But because talented people who can work well together are in short supply, they're in a position to be extremely selective about membership in their circle. Being seen as an attractive team member is an enormous economic advantage, but it's a status that must be earned. If you're a creep, few teams will want you.

Talent and willingness to work hard are obviously positive qualities in a teammate, and members of elite teams rarely lack them. But those qualities aren't sufficient. Successful teamwork also presumes an ability to trust one's colleagues, to believe they'll put the team's interests ahead of their own even when no one is looking. So being selected for membership of an elite team also depends heavily on character assessment.

Character assessment makes little sense in the models of human behavior favored by many economists. Those models assume that people are both rational and self-interested (in the narrow sense of the latter term). In this portrayal, *Homo economicus* would cheat only if he stood to benefit by enough and if the odds of being caught were sufficiently low. So the mere fact that he does not have a reputation for being a cheat tells us only that he's been prudent. It doesn't tell us that he wouldn't cheat when no one is looking.

Now, self-interest is clearly an important human motive, perhaps even the most important one. When speeding fines increase, motorists drive more slowly. When fuel prices rise, people turn down their thermostats and buy more fuel-efficient cars. Yet self-interest cannot be the only important motive. People tip at about the standard rate, for example, even when dining in restaurants they will never visit again.[3] They often donate anonymously to charity and return lost wallets with the cash intact.[4]

Someone trying to assemble an effective team would of course find it extremely useful to be able to predict whether a prospective member would put his own interests ahead of the team's when no one was looking. Are such predictions possible? Consider the following simple thought experiment:

> Imagine that you have just returned from a crowded concert to discover that you have lost $10,000 in cash. The cash had been in an envelope with your name and address on it that apparently fell from your coat pocket while you were at the concert. Do you know anyone not related to you by blood or marriage who you feel certain would return your money?

Whoever finds your envelope confronts a "golden opportunity":[5] to keep the money with essentially no chance of being detected and punished. Yet most people insist they can name others who would be sure to return their money. Most often, the people they name are close friends. It's extremely unlikely that they've had prior opportunities to observe what those friends would do under the circumstances described. So what makes them so confident about their predictions? When pressed, most explain that they know their friends well enough to feel certain they would feel terrible at the mere thought of keeping the money.

Evidence suggests that the intuitions behind these judgments are informative. Along with my colleagues Tom Gilovich and Dennis Regan, I have done laboratory experiments that give subjects an opportunity to play a game in which they and their partners can cheat without the possibility of detection.[6] In these experiments, subjects who met for the first time began with an opportunity to talk for thirty minutes in groups of three. Each subject then went to a separate room to fill out two forms, one for each of the other two subjects in the group. On these forms they indicated whether or not they would cheat in a simple game with small monetary stakes, and they also predicted whether they thought their partners would cheat. Subjects actually cheated in less than a quarter of instances, yet when subjects predicted that a partner would cheat, their predictions were accurate almost 60 percent of the time.

If people are reasonably adept at character assessment, then, the best way to be perceived as an attractive team member may be to become the kind of person who actually is an attractive team member. As psychologists have long understood, humans are creatures of habit, which means that traits of character can actually be cultivated through deliberate repetition. If your goal were to become an attractive teammate, what traits of character would you want to cultivate? This is an important question. As I tell my MBA students, the supervisors who will decide on their future promotions would, if asked, have an opinion about whether they would return a lost envelope containing $10,000.

I urge my students to consider the possibility that their attitudes toward luck may affect how others view them. Because chance events figure prominently along virtually every career trajectory, people who claim complete responsibility for their own success are almost surely claiming more credit than they actually deserve, a move that's unlikely to make them more attractive to others. As Adam Smith wrote, "The man who esteems himself as he ought, and no more than he ought, seldom fails to obtain from other people all the esteem that he himself thinks due. He desires no more than is due to him, and he rests upon it with complete satisfaction."[7]

I also remind my students that most cultures, especially those in the West, celebrate ambition as a personal quality, and that members of successful teams generally possess that quality in abundance. But most cultures also recognize that beyond a certain point, ambition can become a liability. When the desire to get ahead becomes too intense, it can lead people to put their own narrow interests ahead of the team's. Perceptions that someone is "too ambitious" may sometimes be rooted in jealousy or envy, but unusually ambitious individuals can threaten team cohesion even in the absence of such emotions.

Many believe, for example, that former Apple senior vice president Scott Forstall was discharged from his post for that reason. Forstall had been the chief architect of the iOS operating system that powers the iPhone and iPad, whose meteoric sales growth made Apple the most profitable company in history. He had been the longtime protégé of Apple cofounder Steve Jobs, was universally acknowledged as an extraordinary engineering talent, and was sometimes mentioned as a potential future Apple CEO. Yet few press accounts of him during his heyday at the company failed to mention that he was unusually ambitious. According to *Bloomberg Business*, some associates described him off the record as someone who "routinely takes credit for collaborative successes, deflects blame for mistakes."[8] When Forstall was dismissed in October 2012, Apple CEO Tim Cook explained that the move was necessary to preserve the company's collaborative culture.[9]

Does willingness to acknowledge the contributions of others—to admit that your success stemmed in part from what others did—affect your attractiveness as a teammate? My experience with former Fed chairman Ben Bernanke, with whom I had the privilege of coauthoring an introductory economics textbook, suggests that it does. Ben is by far the most successful economist I've ever worked with closely. In addition to his tenure as chair at the Fed, he served as editor of the prestigious *American Economic Review* and was for many years the chairman of Princeton's highly ranked department of economics. He served with distinction in those posts not just because of his intelligence and appetite for hard work—traits possessed by many economists—but also because of other personal qualities that are considerably less common.

Before our book was published, I would occasionally run into economists from Princeton at conferences. And when I'd tell them I was working on a book with Ben, they would invariably volunteer praise for what a fabulous department chairman he'd been. Experienced academics can attest that faculty members rarely express such views about their chairmen.

Most chairmen of academic departments accept their positions only reluctantly and don't try to do much while in office. Chairmen in that mold seldom elicit strong reactions from their department members. In rare instances, however, chairmen energetically try to change their departments, and in most of these cases their subordinates are quick to offer negative judgments. Ben was an extremely active chairman at Princeton, overseeing the recruitment of more than ten new faculty members. Yet he suffered virtually none of the negative fallout from the clashing opinions that surround almost all external faculty appointments.

Although he was often the smartest person in the room, even when the room was full of distinguished academics, he felt absolutely no need for others to perceive him that way. Understanding that good ideas were more likely to be embraced the more widely credit could be shared for them, Ben was always quick to cite the contributions of others.

Those traits surely help explain not only his ability to muster support for controversial faculty appointments at Princeton, but also his ability to rally the support of initially skeptical colleagues at the Fed during the aftermath of the 2008 financial crisis. Many on the Fed's Board of Governors were sympathetic to austerity advocates who argued for tight money and higher interest rates as the best way to restore investor confidence. But one of Ben's academic specialties had been a historical analysis of the Great Depression, and that work had persuaded him that austerity not only would not be helpful, but it would actually deepen the slump. With total spending still far below the level required to put people back to work, he argued, the economy needed vigorous fiscal and monetary stimulus. He couldn't deliver fiscal stimulus, which was in the hands of a Congress determined to take only limited action. But he persuaded many initially reluctant Fed colleagues to back his proposals for the most aggressive monetary expansion our central bank has ever undertaken. Most macroeconomists now agree that without Bernanke's leadership, the Great Recession would have been even deeper and more stubbornly enduring.

One last point about Ben: In economics, it's common for the coauthors of books and papers to be listed alphabetically, and Ben's high professional visibility might have generated additional sales of our book had we followed that convention. Yet he insisted to our publisher that my name go first. It wouldn't seem fair, he explained, for him to be listed first, since he joined the project only after I had already outlined the book's rationale and written drafts of the microeconomics chapters for which I was primarily responsible.

Characterizing what makes someone an attractive teammate is obviously a complex task. I hope we can agree, however, that people who claim too much credit for their accomplishments are properly viewed with skepticism, and that those who insist that luck played no role in their own success are almost surely claiming more than their due.

How do others react to such people? To explore this question further, I conducted an online survey in which I asked two groups of subjects to read contrasting versions of an excerpt of an interview with Harold Johnson, a highly successful biotechnology entrepreneur. Although the excerpt was described as having come from a segment on *60 Minutes*, Johnson is in fact a hypothetical person. The details of his story are completely fictional.

The interviews were written at my request by Kirsten Saracini, an MFA student in Cornell's creative writing program and a family friend. I asked her to portray Johnson as highly competent and confident, if not especially likable. The two versions she prepared were identical except for their concluding paragraphs. The common portion read as follows:

Q: Can you give us a brief history of how you went from doing administrative work at Ohio State University to running the H. J. Institute?

A: Well, I took that job in Columbus so I could take some basic chem for free at the university. I used to hide my books under a stack of manila envelopes—take them out whenever my cubicle mate wasn't paying much attention, whenever I didn't have too much work. So that's the real beginning. Eventually I got my BS in biochemistry from OSU and went on to get my PhD in pharmacology from Yale. You know they pay you to do that if you teach freshmen how to light a Bunsen burner without frying their hair off? You probably know that.

I managed to publish a few papers while I was at Yale, so Harvard expressed some interest in me and my work. I expressed a little interest back and got hired, got tenured, and got bored, all in a little over a decade. That was the 1990s for me. Then I got a plush job with my own research team at the National Institutes of Health. We were doing some work with action potentials in neuronal firing when I started getting distracted by a side project we'd discovered with mRNAs. The NIH expressed some mild interest but they were taking too long to approve the project, get funding, yada yada, so once my contract was up, I was out of there.

My partner and I founded the H. J. Institute soon after I delivered a paper at a conference at Berkeley. A group of investors approached us after that conference and laid out this whole elaborate business plan for raising twenty million in under a year to set up labs, hire some solid, good people, you know. About three years later, we had a patent that a few drug companies needed. They paid us some pretty pennies to use it, so we were able to do some real inspiring and interesting work instead of just chasing around the market. We've been flying high ever since.

In the final paragraph of what I'll call the skill version of the interview, Johnson emphasized that his company's success was primarily a consequence of skill and hard work:

But success didn't just fall into our laps. We've worked hard, and my partner's experience and market intuition were undoubtedly important factors. But lots of people work hard, and lots of MBAs are market-savvy. The real breakthroughs in our lab were highly technical, and I'm probably the only one who could have made them happen.

In the luck version, Johnson said nothing further about his skill and effort. Instead, he noted that his company might not have been nearly as successful except for a few lucky breaks:

We've worked hard, but we've also been lucky. I got to speak at that Berkeley conference only because another speaker canceled at the last minute. If those investors hadn't happened to be there, if they hadn't seen some promise in the work, I don't know if any of the real magic in our lab would've happened.

One or the other of these versions was assigned at random to two groups of roughly three hundred subjects recruited online through Amazon's MTurk service. One group read only the luck version, the other only the skill version. The instructions preceding the excerpts, which were the same for each version, read as follows:

What follows is an excerpt from Morley Safer's 60 Minutes *interview with Harold Johnson, co-founder and CEO of the H. J. Institute, which was named* Biotechnology Magazine's *Company of the year in 2013. After reading the excerpt, please answer the short list of questions on the following page.*

Those questions, and the instructions for responding to them, read as follows:

For each of the three questions below, indicate your likelihood by inserting a hash mark on the 10-point scale shown. Above the hash mark in each case, please write the corresponding number (7.6, for example).

1. If you were the head of a much larger company than Johnson's and had an opportunity to hire him as a senior vice president, how likely would you be to do so?

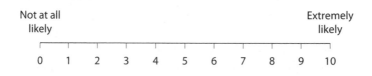

2. How likely do you believe Harold Johnson would be to agree with the following statement: "Kindness toward other people is important."

3. If you and Harold Johnson were neighbors, how likely do you think it would be that you and he would become close friends?

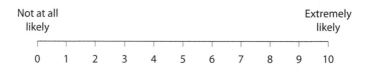

The purpose of these questions was merely to probe subjects' feelings about a highly successful entrepreneur based on his brief account of his path to success. The two versions were word-for-word the same for more than three hundred words, differing only in their final paragraph of less than sixty words. In the final paragraph of the skill version, Johnson credits his success to skill and hard work—a thoroughly plausible attribution to which most reasonable people would not object. Nor would many object to the final paragraph of the luck version, in which Johnson acknowledges that he also benefited from a bit of luck.

It might seem, then, that subjects would find no compelling basis for offering different answers to the questions posed above. My conjecture, however, was that subjects who read the luck version would on balance be more favorably disposed toward Harold Johnson than would those who read the skill version. And in an early pilot study in which the subjects were MBA students, that's indeed what we found. On each of the three questions listed above, subjects who read the luck version of the interview responded significantly more favorably to Harold Johnson than those who read the skill version.

In the follow-up study involving subjects recruited online, the differences in response pattern were smaller and less consistent. For the question of whether respondents would hire Johnson, female subjects reported a higher average likelihood in the luck version than in the skill version, but the pattern was reversed for male subjects. When male and female responses were pooled for this question, there was no significant difference between the average skill and luck responses. Dividing the subject pool into those with bachelor's or higher degrees and all others produced a similar pattern for this question: More-educated subjects said they would be more likely to hire Johnson in the luck version than in the skill version, but the response pattern was reversed for less-educated subjects. Here, too, the differences were not statistically significant.

Responses to the second and third questions tracked my expectations much more closely. As shown in figure 8.1, subjects

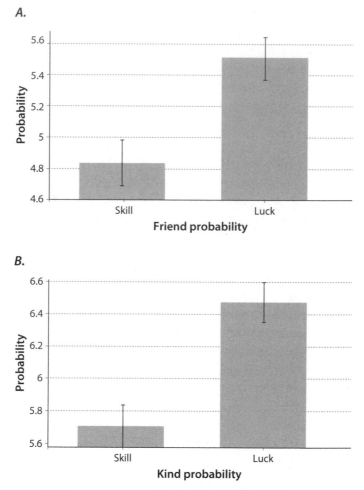

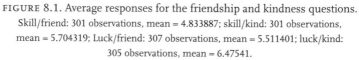

FIGURE 8.1. Average responses for the friendship and kindness questions. Skill/friend: 301 observations, mean = 4.833887; skill/kind: 301 observations, mean = 5.704319; Luck/friend: 307 observations, mean = 5.511401; luck/kind: 305 observations, mean = 6.47541.

who read the luck version of the interview reported both a higher average likelihood of becoming friends with Johnson and a higher average likelihood that he would believe that kindness toward others was important, just as in the earlier pilot study. For these two questions, response patterns were essentially the same for both male and female subjects and for both more- and less-educated subjects.

So although the differences were modest and not entirely consistent, subjects who read the version of the interview in which Johnson acknowledged luck's role in his success had a generally more favorable opinion of the man. They thought that they'd be more likely to befriend him and that he'd be more likely to value kindness toward others, suggesting they saw the Johnson portrayed in the luck version as the more attractive potential teammate. These findings are also in line with the conventional view that modesty, within limits, is an attractive personal quality.

In short, it may be in your interest to acknowledge luck's role in your success if only because people will think better of you for having done so. Evidence suggests that this will make you feel happier. And by making you a more attractive potential teammate, the mere fact that others think better of you may also make you more likely to prosper in purely material terms.

As I've noted, the widespread human tendency to attribute success to skill and effort and failure to bad luck may be psychologically adaptive in some cases. But on balance, I believe it's in our interest to embrace more realistic attributions. Just as it may be often in our interest to acknowledge luck's role in our successes, we might also do well to invoke the excuse of bad luck a little less frequently. For example, I would have been better off, I'm sure, if I'd spent fewer years regretting my misfortune at having my dream of becoming a Major League Baseball player shattered prematurely.

As a boy, baseball was almost all I cared about. Up through my final year of eligibility for Little League competition in South Florida, I practiced hitting and fielding during almost every available daylight hour. Thanks to a well-connected friend, I'd been hired as ball boy by the then Brooklyn Dodgers for their annual ten-game spring exhibition series at Miami Stadium. For two seasons, I got to spend long hours with Dodger stars like PeeWee Reese, Roy Campanella, and Sandy Koufax. What a thrill it was to listen to their stories and bask in their encouragement! I was certain that baseball was the life I was destined to live.

At age thirteen, however, I'd bought a motorcycle, and the jobs I worked in order to pay for it forced me to drop out of organized competition. Two years later, the motorcycle was history, and I decided to take up baseball again. In the meantime, I'd moved to a different school district so wasn't part of the pipeline that fed into my new school's team. Still, on the first day of practice, I cleanly fielded every ball that was hit my way, threw accurately, and hit many balls sharply during batting practice. The following day, however, I got word that I hadn't been selected for the team.

I was crushed, and for many years afterward felt deep regret about having foolishly dropped out of baseball for those two years. I'd been a good player, I thought, and if I'd continued, I felt sure I'd have ended up in the big leagues.

Once I began studying winner-take-all markets as a professional economist, however, I began to understand how naïve that expectation had been. The numbers tell a dramatically different story from the one I'd envisioned as a boy. Even if I'd continued playing and had done well in high school competition, I probably wouldn't have been drafted by a professional team. But even if I had been, the overwhelmingly likely outcome would have been to have ridden a bus in the minor leagues for ten years before realizing I'd never make it in the majors.

In that case, I'd have found myself a twenty-eight-year-old with only a high school diploma having to figure out what to do in life. As things turned out, however, I was teaching economics at Cornell University at twenty-eight, having earned my PhD a year earlier. All things considered, then, lamenting my blown chance to continue playing baseball was a colossal waste of energy.

♠

In the normal course of events, few of us give much thought to how seemingly minor random events often profoundly alter our lives. Failure to give luck its due is of course not the only reason we've failed to maintain the environments that so many of us have been fortunate enough to enjoy. But it's been a contributing factor. The good news is that some relatively simple changes in public policy would free up the resources we need to restore those environments without demanding painful sacrifices from anyone.

My argument for change is one that appeals directly to self-interest. We could bring individual spending incentives into much closer alignment with society's broader interests simply by scrapping our current income tax in favor of a much more steeply progressive tax on each family's annual consumption expenditure. That step would reduce the recent high rates of spending growth for mansions, cars, jewelry, and celebrations of special occasions. Not a shred of evidence suggests that such a change would make top earners any less happy. If all mansions were a little smaller, all cars a little less expensive, all diamonds a little more modest, and all celebrations a little less costly, the standards that define "special" in each case would adjust accordingly, leaving successful people just as happy as before.

This point is important to bear in mind when weighing one of the most common objections to any proposal that would generate additional tax revenue: People often say they'd be willing to pay higher taxes in support of public goods except for their fear that government would simply waste the money. But even though there are indeed bridges to nowhere and other clear examples of government waste, most people concede that a large portion of the government's budget is spent on public goods and services that actually deliver real value. That's in stark contrast to the growth we've seen in private consumption at the highest levels, much of which is squandered in fruitless positional arms races. Contrary to popular belief, private waste is not only far more pervasive than government waste, but also far easier to curtail.

The upshot is that wealthy citizens with even the most jaundiced view of government should regard the adoption of a progressive consumption tax as an essentially risk-free step. At least *some* useful public goods would be purchased with the additional revenue, after all, and unless someone is prepared to argue that another tripling of the amounts spent on weddings would make people happier, virtually nothing of value would be sacrificed.

As the political scientist Robert Putnam has argued in *Our Kids*, there is also a compelling moral case for rebuilding the environments that foster success.[10] Relying in part on case studies of families in his hometown of Port Clinton, Ohio, Putnam illustrates how growing income gaps have profoundly diminished the opportunities available to low-income children. His case studies are bolstered by more systematic data from the Educational Longitudinal Survey by the Department of Educa-

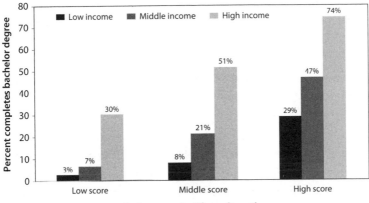

FIGURE 8.2. Educational attainment and socioeconomic status.
Source: M. A. Fox, B. A. Connolly, and T. D. Snyder, "Youth Indicators 2005: Trends in the Well-Being of American Youth," Washington, DC, US Department of Education, National Center for Education Statistics, table 21, http://nces.ed.gov/pubs2005/2005050.pdf.

tion. Getting ahead without a college education has become an increasingly formidable challenge, and that's been a devastating blow to the children of low-income families. As reflected in figure 8.2, for example, the children from those families with eighth-grade math scores in the top quartile are actually less likely to earn a bachelor's degree than the children of high-income families with bottom-quartile math scores.[11] And with college tuition rising faster than even the cost of medical care, children of low-income families who do manage to earn their degrees are graduating with crushing student loan burdens.

Politicians on both sides of the aisle celebrate the American Dream, the ideal that talented people who work hard and play by the rules can get ahead, irrespective of their family backgrounds. As Putnam argues persuasively, that dream is now in tatters. Few people can feel proud that the barriers to success have become so much more formidable for the children of poor families. And since we can easily afford to do something about this, how can we justify continued inaction?

Putnam has been a friend for many years, and we discussed our current book projects when I met with him over coffee during a visit to Cambridge in the fall of 2014. I explained why I thought the kinds of public investments we were both advocating would be more likely to happen if the wealthy realized that those investments would benefit not only the poor but themselves as well. Without contesting the point, Bob argued that significant social change was almost always precipitated by moral arguments rather than ones based on narrow self-interest. He added that his hope for *Our Kids* was that it would help ignite the moral conversation necessary to prompt political action. I said that I shared his hope but wondered whether moral arguments alone would be sufficient to overcome the influence of big money in today's political climate. The wealthy have developed moral reasons of their own for not taking the steps we advocate, and they now have extremely large megaphones.

The important point, however, is that in this case there simply is no conflict between morality and self-interest. Yes, there are compelling moral arguments for increasing our investment in our children's future; but as I have stressed, those very same investments will promote the narrow interests of the wealthy citizens who must pay a disproportionate share of their cost.

Indeed, a long-standing theme in my own work has been that the conflict between morality and self-interest is less severe than many presume. In a 1988 book, for example, I used the thought experiment described earlier in this chapter to illustrate how genuinely honest people might prosper in even the most bitterly competitive environments.[12] In situations that require trust, people who can be trusted are extremely valuable.

If we can indeed identify such people, as the thought experiment suggests, their premium pay can adequately compensate them for any gains they forgo by not cheating. Change is always difficult. But failing to change sometimes entails even greater difficulty. By living in private gated communities and taking other forms of evasive action, successful people have been able to escape some of the consequences of recent sharp cutbacks in infrastructure spending. But many other consequences have been impossible to escape. It's not practical, for example, to take every short journey by helicopter. Nor does being wealthy insulate you from the hazards and discomforts of congested airports and poorly maintained public roadways. Owning a factory doesn't insulate you from our schools' failure to produce enough qualified workers.

Congress as currently constituted is of course unlikely to consider the adoption of any new taxes. But with tens of millions of additional retirements looming, the country will be awash in debt unless we can find new sources of revenue. We could wait for the inevitable financial crisis to occur. Or we could start talking now about why it would make sense to take action more quickly.

In light of my personal history, I count myself fortunate not just to be alive, but to be able to participate in this conversation. Things could have so easily turned out differently. Sudden cardiac arrest deprives the brain of oxygen, which probably explains why I was unable to form new memories during the first several days following my collapse on the tennis court on that mid-November morning in 2007. You can only imagine my family's profound relief when that problem suddenly seemed to vanish on day four. (I'd have been profoundly relieved myself except that I wasn't even aware I had a problem.) Still unresolved at the time, however, was whether I might have suffered any enduring cognitive deficits of a more subtle sort.

To see where I stood, I went in January 2008 for a follow-up visit with the neurologist who'd examined me when I was in the hospital. One of the tests he'd given me in November was to ask whether I could remember three simple words—hat, shoe, and pen—that he'd asked me to hold in mind a few minutes earlier. Family members tell me that I couldn't recall any of them, or even that he'd asked me to hold three words in mind.

In the ensuing weeks, as evidence of my recovery continued to accumulate, my incompetence at this task became a running joke in the family. One of my Christmas presents from my wife and our sons was a box titled "the great triumvirate." They asked me to guess what three things were in the box. Of course, I had no idea. When I opened it to find a Tilley hat, a Cross pen, and a tiny tennis shoe that Ellen had molded out of clay, they explained that these were the three words the neurologist had asked me about.

On the morning before going for my follow-up visit with the neurologist, I asked Ellen to test me with three new words. "Tree, box, squirrel," she said, then asked me five minutes later whether I could recite them. Before answering, I asked whether

Hat, shoe, pen

she could remember them. She could not. (This test is harder than it seems!) But I was relieved that I could.

About fifteen minutes into my session with the neurologist that afternoon, he told me he was going to ask me to remember three words. It was all Ellen and I could do to keep from cracking up when he used the same three words he had in November—hat, shoe, and pen! (Of course he would use the same words every time. How else could HE remember them?) When he asked whether I could recall them five minutes later, I momentarily drew a blank. But then the image of the hat, shoe, and pen in my Christmas gift box flashed before my eyes, and I was out of there with a clean bill of health.

With the extra time I've been granted, I've continued trying to explain why a few relatively simple changes in policy could produce dramatic improvements for all of us. If the ideas I've presented here make sense to you, I hope you'll discuss them with others. If we're to change course, it will be because of conversations like these. Be encouraged, as I have been, that public opinion on any subject emerges from a complex dynamic process in which what people deem reasonable to believe depends in part on what their conversation partners believe. The upshot is that although popular beliefs may remain at odds with reality for considerable periods of time, the consensus can flip with surprising speed once good arguments begin to find their footing. And those arguments can spread only one conversation at a time.

APPENDIX 1

DETAILED SIMULATION RESULTS
FOR CHAPTER 4

This appendix provides a more detailed description of the simulations discussed in chapter 4, which explore the role of small random influences on contest outcomes.[1] Each simulated contest takes the form of a winner-take-all tournament whose outcome depends only on performance. Performance is objectively measurable, and whichever contestant has the highest total performance score wins.

To help get a feel for the slightly more detailed examples to follow, I'll start with a simpler one in which performance depends only on skill and in which each contestant's skill is denoted by a random number that's equally likely to lie anywhere between 0 and 100.

For this simple distribution, the average skill level is 50:

0   50   100

Skill level

As more people enter the contest, we'll see a broader range of observed skill levels across contestants. That means that the more contestants there are, the more dispersed their skill levels will be and hence the higher the highest skill level among them will be:

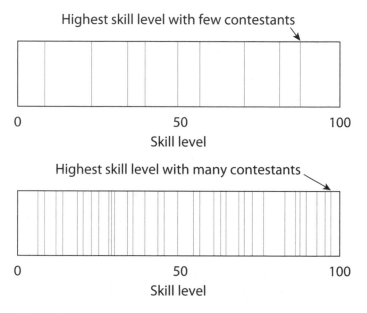

Highest skill level with few contestants

Highest skill level with many contestants

If we observed thousands of contests, each with only two contestants, the average skill level of the better of the two would be 66.7. The average skill level of the lesser of the two would be 33.3.

Similarly, the average skill level of the best of three contestants would be 75:

0   25   50   75   100

Skill level

And the average skill level of the best of four contestants would be 80:

0   20   40   60   80   100

Skill level

More generally, the average value of the highest skill level observed in a contest with N contestants would be $100[N/(N + 1)]$:

0   50   100

Skill level $100 \times \dfrac{N}{N+1}$

For this example, the expected highest skill level climbs steadily with the number of contestants, but once the number of contestants grows large, the gains become extremely small:

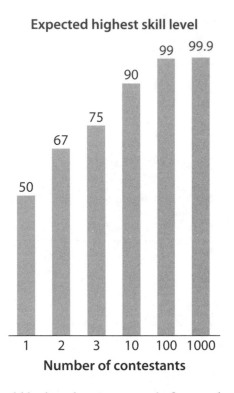

Expected highest skill level

1	2	3	10	100	1000
50	67	75	90	99	99.9

Number of contestants

Now let's add luck to the picture. As before, each contestant's skill is a random number equally likely to take any value between 0 and 100. But this time performance depends not only on skill but also on luck, which is also a random number equally likely to take any value between 0 and 100. To portray the relative importance of skill and luck, I'll assume that each contestant's performance is a weighted sum of skill and luck values, with most of the weight on skill, and only a small amount on luck. For instance, if we suppose that performance depends 95 percent on skill and only 5 percent on luck, a candidate with, say, a skill level of 90 and a luck level of 60 would have a performance level of $0.95 \times 90 + 0.05 \times 60 = 88.5$, only slightly below that person's skill level.

Since luck is an inherently random concept, the most natural assumption is that skill and luck are not correlated. So the most skilled contestant is no more likely to be lucky than anyone else. For example, the most skillful competitor in a field of 1,000 would have an expected skill level of 99.9, but an expected luck level of only 50.

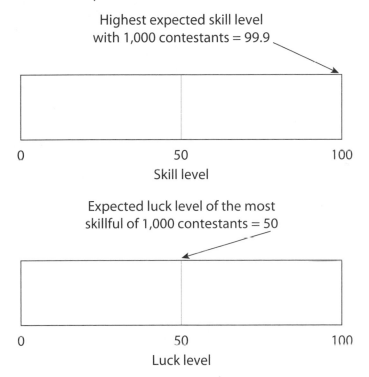

Highest expected skill level
with 1,000 contestants = 99.9

0   50   100
Skill level

Expected luck level of the most
skillful of 1,000 contestants = 50

0   50   100
Luck level

It follows that the expected performance level of the most skillful of 1,000 contestants is $P = 0.95 \times 99.9 + 0.05 \times 50 = 97.4$, which is only 2.6 points below the maximum value. But with 999 other contestants, that score usually won't be good enough to win.

With 1,000 contestants, we expect that 10 will have skill levels of 99 or higher. Among those 10, the highest expected luck level is $(10/11) \times 100 = 90.9$. The highest expected performance score among 1,000 contestants must therefore be at least P = $0.95 \times 99 + 0.05 \times 90.9 = 98.6$, which is 1.2 points higher than the expected performance score of the most skillful contestant.

In short, with 1,000 contestants, there will almost always be one who is nearly as talented as the most talented contestant but also significantly luckier. The upshot is that even when luck counts for only a tiny fraction of total performance, the winner of a large contest will seldom be the most skillful contestant but will usually be one of the luckiest.

The figures below describe the results of some additional simulations in which performance depends on three factors: ability, effort, and luck. In these examples, ability and effort count equally and together make up the lion's share of any con-

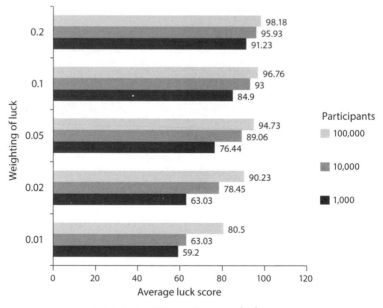

FIGURE A1.1. Winners' average luck scores.

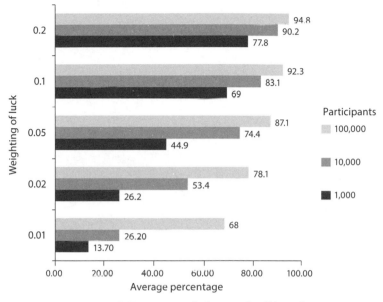

FIGURE A1.2. Percentage of winners who did NOT have the highest ability + effort score.

testant's performance total. Luck's share of performance varies across the examples, with weights ranging from 1 to 20 percent. For each set of weights, I also allow the number of contestants to vary, ranging from 1,000 to 100,000. The number of contests in each simulation is 1,000. All the scores for ability, effort, and luck are real numbers that are equally likely to take any value between 0 and 100.

Figure A1.1 reports the winners' average luck scores for these simulations, and figure A1.2 reports the percentage of winners who did NOT rank first in the ability + effort score among their fellow contestants.

APPENDIX 2

FREQUENTLY ASKED QUESTIONS ABOUT THE PROGRESSIVE CONSUMPTION TAX

WHAT'S THE DIFFERENCE BETWEEN A PROGRESSIVE CONSUMPTION TAX AND OTHER FORMS OF CONSUMPTION TAXES, SUCH AS THE SALES TAX AND VALUE-ADDED TAX?

Value-added taxes are similar to the familiar sales taxes levied in most states. Recent proposals to adopt a "flat tax" call for replacing the current income tax with a national sales tax. With sales taxes, which are normally levied at the cash register, buyers pay a fixed percentage of the pre-tax sales prices of goods they purchase. A value-added tax is, as its name suggests, a tax levied on the price increase that occurs at each stage as goods move through the production process. Functionally, value-added taxes are essentially equivalent to standard sales taxes. In each case buyers end up paying a tax that is a fixed percentage of the price of whatever they buy.

In contrast, a progressive consumption tax is not levied at the cash register or at each stage of the production process, nor is it a fixed percentage of the price of each good purchased. Like the familiar income tax, it is paid once each year, but instead of being levied on taxable income, it is levied on taxable consumption. Taxable consumption, in turn, is calculated as taxable income minus annual additions to savings minus a large standard deduction. For example, if a family had taxable income of $60,000 for the year, and if its savings balance had grown by $10,000 during the year, and if the annual standard deduction was $30,000, taxable consumption for the year would be $60,000 − 10,000 − $30,000 = $20,000.

Once the family has computed its taxable consumption, the amount of tax it owes would be found in a table published by the tax authorities (just as the family would currently consult such a table to discover how much income tax it owes). With a progressive income tax, the rate levied on the first dollars a family earns is low, and rates on additional income then rise gradually. Under a progressive income tax, similarly, rates would also start off low and then rise gradually as taxable consumption increases.

Since the progressive consumption tax exempts savings from taxation, the marginal tax rates on the highest consumption levels would have to be higher than under the current income tax in order to maintain current tax revenue levels.

HOW WOULD BORROWING AND LOAN REPAYMENTS BE HANDLED UNDER A PROGRESSIVE CONSUMPTION TAX?

Loans taken out during any given year would be treated for tax purposes as negative savings. If our hypothetical family with taxable income of $60,000 and annual savings of $10,000, had also taken out a new loan for $5,000 during the tax year, its taxable consumption for the year (assuming the same standard deduction of $30,000) would be $60,000 − $10,000 + $5,000 − $30,000 = $25,000, or $5,000 more than if it had not taken out the loan. Loan repayments would be treated symmetrically—that is, as equivalent to positive savings.

HOW WOULD PURCHASES OF HOUSES AND OTHER EXPENSIVE DURABLES BE TREATED UNDER A PROGRESSIVE CONSUMPTION TAX?

Because houses last a long time, a family that buys a $1 million house in a given tax year actually increases its consumption of housing services by only a small fraction of that amount during that year. It would therefore be necessary to spread out such large durable expenditures over many years, much as the current tax system now does for many types of business investment. With a twenty-year smoothing scheme, for example, a $1 million house purchase would be counted as $50,000 of consumption during each of the next twenty years.

AREN'T CONSUMPTION TAXES EXTREMELY REGRESSIVE?

Conventional sales and value-added taxes are indeed highly regressive, for the simple reason that high-income families save at significantly higher rates than other families. The main objection to flat taxes and other sales taxes is their regressivity (although proponents of flat taxes have offered proposals—mainly to exempt basic necessities from taxation—that would make them less regressive). The progressive consumption tax, by design, is not a regressive tax. On the contrary, its rate structure can be adjusted to achieve any degree of desired progressivity.

WOULDN'T TAXING CONSUMPTION INHIBIT SPENDING, CAUSING
THE ECONOMY TO SLOW DOWN?

Yes, but only if the economy was sluggish to begin with. The
basic problem plaguing an economy operating at less than full
employment is that low levels of total spending enable producers to serve their customers without having to hire everyone
who wants to work. So, by making the after-tax price of consumer goods higher, taxing consumption would indeed inhibit
spending, exacerbating an already sluggish economy. Since the
economies of most nations have not yet recovered fully from
the global financial crisis of 2008, adoption of a progressive consumption tax should be postponed until full employment has
again been restored.

Once that happens, the progressive consumption tax should
be phased in slowly, allowing it to gradually replace the income
tax. As people responded by increasing their savings slightly,
the effect at first would be to produce a small reduction in the
share of national output consumed. At the same, the availability of additional savings would cause interest rates to fall, which
would give firms an incentive to increase their investment spending. For each dollar by which consumption went down, then,
investment would go up by a dollar, leaving total spending the
same as before. An economy's ability to achieve full employment depends on its total spending, not on how that total is
apportioned between consumption and investment. So a progressive consumption tax would not cause the economy to slow
down, provided it was already operating at full employment.

On the contrary, the progressive consumption tax would actually stimulate long-term economic growth in a fully employed
economy. With higher investment and lower consumption, more
workers would be employed to produce investment goods and
fewer to produce consumer goods. Over time, higher investment

would increase worker productivity, leading to higher wages and more rapid growth in national income. Once national income grew sufficiently, the total amount of consumption in the economy would actually exceed what it would have been under the income tax (even though consumption would constitute a smaller proportion of total output).

HOW COULD THE TRANSITION FROM THE CURRENT SYSTEM BEST BE MANAGED?

Legislators in a sluggish economy could greatly accelerate the recovery of total spending levels by adopting a progressive consumption tax right away, but announcing that its gradual phase-in would begin only after the economy was back at full employment. High-income families that were thinking about building bigger mansions or staging expensive celebrations in the future would want to accelerate those purchases, thereby escaping the tax. Hundreds of billions of dollars of additional consumption spending would produce immediate economic stimulus without requiring any additional government spending.

It might be better still, of course, to stimulate the economy by accelerating long overdue infrastructure spending. But if that's not a possibility, inducing the wealthy to build bigger mansions would be better than inaction.

HOW WOULD SWITCHING TO A PROGRESSIVE CONSUMPTION TAX AFFECT THE GOVERNMENT'S ABILITY TO STIMULATE THE ECONOMY DURING RECESSIONS?

The government's challenge in a depressed economy is to stimulate spending by whatever means it can. One way is to increase government spending directly. A second way is for central banks to stimulate investment spending by reducing interest rates.

And under the current income tax, a third way is to stimulate consumption spending by cutting income taxes temporarily.

Unfortunately, temporary income tax cuts are a weak stimulus measure in practice because consumers tend to save their extra disposable income rather than spend it. Saving more is a rational response in the face of employment uncertainty but does nothing to stimulate a depressed economy.

An economy operating under a progressive consumption tax has a much more powerful stimulus remedy at its disposal. That's because the only way consumers can benefit from a temporary reduction in the progressive consumption tax is by spending more money right away. They'll receive no benefit from any consumption they postpone until after the temporary cut has expired.

WHY WOULDN'T IT BE BETTER TO IMPOSE CONSUMPTION TAXES ONLY ON LUXURY ITEMS?

Many societies have imposed taxes on specific luxury items in an effort to curb spending seen as wasteful, but in practice these taxes have generally proved counterproductive. The problem is that the concept of luxury is highly elastic. If one good is taxed as a luxury, consumers can simply shift to untaxed goods that satisfy the same basic desires. Centuries ago, for example, a country taxed buttons of gold, only to see the wealthy switch to buttons of carved ivory. Another problem is that taxing specific goods as luxuries all but guarantees a legislative quagmire, as lobbyists for each industry attempt to persuade Congress that its particular product is a necessity that should be exempt.

Taxing total expenditure at progressive rates does not require Congress to make judgments about which goods are luxuries, nor does it create incentives for consumers to switch to untaxed substitutes. Since high marginal tax rates apply only to expenditures beyond a high threshold, the implied judgment is that such expenditures are rarely for things that most people would regard as necessities.

WOULDN'T IT BE UNFAIR TO TAX RETIREES WHEN THEY CONSUME THEIR SAVINGS, SINCE THEY'VE ALREADY PAID INCOME TAXES ON THE MONEY THEY'VE SAVED?

Yes, and for this reason it would be essential that money saved under the current income tax system be exempt from additional taxation when savings are drawn down during retirement.

WHY WOULDN'T THE EXTREMELY WEALTHY SIMPLY IGNORE THE PROGRESSIVE CONSUMPTION TAX?

It's true that many of today's wealthy could increase their current spending tenfold and still have hundreds of millions remaining in their accounts at death. Although these people could afford to continue spending at their current rates even in the face of a steeply progressive consumption tax, evidence suggests that they would not. Many of Manhattan's wealthiest residents, for example, could afford to buy the entire building that houses their current apartments, yet it is unusual for them to occupy apartments larger than ten thousand square feet. If those same residents lived in Houston or Cleveland, however, most would live in houses larger than twenty thousand square feet. That they choose smaller dwellings in Manhattan is clear evidence that even the wealthy respond to price signals. The per-square-foot cost of Manhattan real estate is more than twice that of the other cities, which has induced most Manhattan residents to settle for smaller apartments. One indirect consequence is that since other Manhattanites are living in smaller spaces, the frame of reference there has shifted so that smaller spaces seem like enough, even for those who could easily afford more.

HOW WOULD A PROGRESSIVE CONSUMPTION TAX SLOW DOWN THE EXPENDITURE CASCADES THAT CREATE FINANCIAL PRESSURE ON THE MIDDLE CLASS?

Since even the wealthy respond to price incentives, a progressive consumption tax would induce those at the top of the income ladder to spend less. They would build smaller additions to their mansions, host less extravagant parties to celebrate special occasions, spend less on automobiles and jewelry, and so on. This would shift the frame of reference that shapes demands of those just below them, who travel in the same social circles, so they too would spend less. This chain of effects would occur all the way down the income ladder. And if other middle-income families were spending less on housing, the pressures that induce any given middle-income family to spend more would also be smaller.

WOULDN'T THE CONSUMPTION TAX LEAD TO MORE WEALTH INEQUALITY, SINCE THE RICH SAVE A HIGHER PROPORTION OF THEIR INCOMES THAN OTHERS DO?

One of the strongest rationales for the progressive consumption tax is that it would reduce consumption inequality, which, as discussed, would eliminate some of the waste inherent in expenditure cascades. But the progressive rate structure would give wealthy households a stronger incentive to increase their savings, which would reinforce their existing tendency to save at higher rates than lower-income households. So, yes, the adoption of a progressive consumption tax would be likely to increase the inequality of household wealth. Historically, two of the most worrisome practical consequences of increased inequality of wealth have been the creation of family dynasties and increased concentration of political power among the wealthy. In weighing the adoption of a progressive consumption tax, societies will therefore want to weigh carefully the adoption of stronger estate taxation and more stringent limits on political campaign contributions.

IS A ROBUST ESTATE TAX A POLITICALLY REALISTIC COMPLEMENT TO THE PROGRESSIVE CONSUMPTION TAX?

Branded as the "death tax" by opponents, the estate tax has been steadily rolled back in recent years, with the exemption level for bequests from parents now set at almost $11 million. Public opinion surveys suggest that estate tax repeal is favored by a majority even of persons in the bottom quintile of the wealth distribution, who face virtually no chance of ever paying estate taxes under current arrangements. So the implementation of a more robust estate tax would indeed appear to represent a formidable challenge.

But when voters are reminded of the fact that eliminating the estate tax would necessitate either significant increases in other taxes or steep reductions in public spending, opposition quickly evaporates. In one survey, for example, when voters were reminded that estate tax repeal would require some combination of higher income or sales taxes and reduced spending on specific public goods, they opposed repeal of the estate tax by more than 4 to 1.[1] In short, opposition to the estate tax quickly evaporates once the alternatives are made clear.

There is actually a strong affirmative case for greater reliance on the estate tax. This tax is closely analogous to the use of lawyers' contingency contracts. Consider someone who is injured by a corporation's negligence but can't afford to hire an attorney. If the case has merit, a lawyer will offer to argue it on a contingency basis: If they lose their suit, the lawyer receives no payment, but if they win, the lawyer receives a percentage of the damages awarded. Note the striking similarity between this arrangement and the terms in effect under an estate tax. Starting out in life, most taxpayers don't know whether they'll end up highly successful, but realists understand that most of them will not. With an estate tax in effect, the government will be able to offer additional public services of value, such as better roads and schools. All taxpayers will enjoy those services, whether or not they end up successful. Their estates will be taxed after death in the unlikely event that they died as multimillionaires. On what grounds might we expect a majority of informed young taxpayers to oppose an arrangement like that?

Budget realists acknowledge that with tens of millions of baby boomers entering retirement, growing budget shortfalls will require additional sources of revenue. And as that reality becomes more widely appreciated, it is reasonable to expect that increased reliance on estate taxes will become increasingly attractive.

Some parents worry that the estate tax would prevent them from ensuring their children's financial security. Yet current exemption levels enable children to inherit more than enough to earn multiple degrees, launch a business, buy a luxury house, and still have several million dollars left for a rainy day. On reflection, would people really want their children to inherit more than that? Long-established wealthy families have traditionally been wary of the corrosive effect of guaranteed wealth on their children's ability to launch successful careers of their own. Early on, the multibillionaire investor Warren Buffett told his children not to expect much of an inheritance, a move for which his son Peter later expressed profound gratitude.[2]

HOW WOULD A PROGRESSIVE CONSUMPTION TAX AFFECT THE
VARIOUS OTHER TAXES WE CURRENTLY LEVY?

A tax on any activity has two effects: it generates revenue and it discourages the activity in question. Most of the other taxes we levy have the undesirable side effect of discouraging useful activities. Since a family's income is its consumption plus its savings, for example, the income tax discourages savings. Because the payroll tax makes it more expensive to take on additional workers, it discourages companies from creating jobs. A strong component of the case for the progressive consumption tax is that its high top marginal rates discourage spending that causes harm to others. Wealthy families of course have no intention of harming others when they build more expensive mansions or stage more expensive celebrations of special occasions. Yet such spending inevitably shifts the frames of reference that govern what families with lower incomes must spend to achieve basic goals.

A rational tax system would abandon all current taxes on useful activities and replace them with taxes on those activities that cause undue harm to others. Such taxes are often called Pigouvian taxes, after the British economist A. C. Pigou, an earlier advocate of their use. For example, since corporate profits, per se, cause no harm to others, the corporate income tax could be replaced by a tax on carbon emissions, which climate scientists believe have already caused enormous harm. We could tax vehicles by weight, since buying heavier vehicles puts others at greater risk of injury and death; we could charge for the use of congested roadways, since entering them causes others to take longer to get where they're going; and so on. In short, the progressive consumption tax is a Pigouvian tax, and a compelling case can be made for replacing existing taxes on useful activities with ones on activities that cause undue harm to others.

IF THE ULTIMATE PURPOSE OF ECONOMIC ACTIVITY IS TO
PRODUCE GOODS AND SERVICES THAT PEOPLE VALUE, WHY WOULD
WE WANT TO LIMIT CONSUMPTION WITH A PROGRESSIVE
CONSUMPTION TAX?

The case for the progressive consumption tax is that it provides
powerful incentives to shift the composition of what we produce in ways that provide greater value than the current mix.
The current mix falls short not because consumers don't know
what's best, but rather because individual incentives are at odds
with what's best collectively. As in the familiar stadium metaphor, it's rational for all to stand to get a better view, yet each
would see just as well if all remained comfortably seated.

IF THE PROGRESSIVE CONSUMPTION TAX IS SUCH A GOOD IDEA,
WHY HAVEN'T WE ALREADY ADOPTED IT?

Most US taxpayers are already operating under a progressive
consumption tax, since only a small percentage of households
save as much as the maximum amounts allowed in existing tax-
deferred retirement accounts like IRAs and 401Ks. But most
wealthy families do not now face the same incentives, since they
save considerably more than those maximum allowances. And
since expenditure cascades start at the top of the income ladder,
the current tax system does nothing to discourage them.

COULD THE PROGRESSIVE CONSUMPTION TAX BE IMPLEMENTED
AT THE STATE OR PROVINCIAL LEVEL?

The ability of people to migrate to adjacent jurisdictions places
constraints on the kinds of tax policies any given state or prov-
ince can adopt in practice. For example, if a state adopted an unusually high income tax, it would risk losing wealthy taxpayers

to nearby states. But a state that adopted a progressive consumption tax could actually attract high-income taxpayers from outside its borders. At the margin, wealthy taxpayers spend their dollars in search of things that seem "special," but special is a relative concept, and the standards that make something special tend to be highly local. If a state adopted a progressive consumption tax, its wealthy residents would have an incentive to save more and spend less on additions to their mansions and coming-of-age parties for their children. But since all would be spending less on such things, the local standards that define special would adjust, making the smaller outlays just as effective as the earlier larger ones had been.

Well-informed wealthy persons would thus have plausible reasons for considering a move to a neighboring state that had adopted a progressive consumption tax. Such a move would enable them to meet expectations without having to spend as much, freeing them to invest more of their hard-earned money. If experience with a progressive consumption tax at the state level proved attractive in this way, other states would also face pressure to adopt progressive consumption taxation, so the first mover's relative advantage would be only temporary.

Better still, of course, would be to adopt the progressive consumption tax at the national level. But political support for such a move would undoubtedly be easier to muster if the policy had already proved successful in several state experiments.

ISN'T THE PROGRESSIVE CONSUMPTION TAX JUST A POLITICAL
PIPE DREAM?

As noted in chapter 7, the progressive consumption tax has a long history of bipartisan support. Senators Pete Domenici (R, NM) and Sam Nunn (D, GA) proposed a progressive consumption tax in 1995, and, although their proposal never came up for a vote, it was not regarded as a radical idea. In an article published in the *American Economic Review* in 1943, longtime University of Chicago free-market advocate Milton Friedman proposed the progressive consumption tax as the most effective way to pay for the World War II effort. And two senior scholars at the American Enterprise Institute, a conservative think tank in Washington, DC, celebrated the virtues of the progressive consumption tax in a recently published book.[3]

An immediate fiscal crisis will probably have to occur before Congress will be willing to take up the issue of comprehensive tax reform in earnest. But with demands for government services poised to continue exceeding sources of federal revenue to pay for them, such a crisis is only a matter of time. And when it does occur, the progressive consumption tax will be high on the list of options under consideration.

NOTES

PREFACE

1. Michael Young, *The Rise of the Meritocracy*, London: Transaction, 1994 (originally published in 1958).
2. Michael Young, "Down with Meritocracy, *Guardian*," June 28, 2001, http://www.theguardian.com/politics/2001/jun/29/comment.
3. Michael Lewis, "Don't Eat Fortune's Cookie," Princeton University's 2012 Baccalaureate Remarks, http://www.princeton.edu/main/news/archive/S33/87/54K53/.
4. Nicholas Kristof, "Is a Hard Life Inherited?," *New York Times*, August 9, 2014, http://www.nytimes.com/2014/08/10/opinion/sunday/nicholas-kristof-is-a-hard-life-inherited.html?_r=0.
5. Nicholas Kristof, "U.S.A., Land of Limitations?," *New York Times*, August 8, 2015, http://www.nytimes.com/2015/08/09/opinion/sunday/nicholas-kristof-usa-land-of-limitations.html.
6. The experiment was part of an ongoing body of experimental work exploring the relationship between status and morality. See Paul K. Piff, Daniel M. Stancato, Stéphane Côté, Rodolfo Mendoza-Denton, and Dacher Keltner, "Higher Social Class Predicts Increased Unethical Behavior," *Proceedings of the National Academy of Sciences* 109.11 (2013): 4086–91, http://www.pnas.org/content/109/11/4086.full.

CHAPTER 1: WRITE WHAT YOU KNOW

1. Robert H. Frank, "Before Tea, Thank Your Lucky Stars," *New York Times*, April 26, 2009, http://www.nytimes.com/2009/04/26/business/economy/26view.html?_r=0.
2. Fox Business News, "Luck Is the Real Key to Success?," May 7, 2011, http://video.foxbusiness.com/v/3887675/luck-is-the-real-key-to-success/#sp=show-clips.

3. Terry Gross, "Fresh Air Remembers the Crime Novelist Elmore Leonard," National Public Radio, August 23, 2013, http://www.npr.org/player/v2/mediaPlayer.html?action=1&t=1&islist=false&id=214831379&m=214836712.

4. Branko Milanovic, "Global Inequality of Opportunity: How Much of Our Income Is Determined by Where We Live?," *Review of Economics and Statistics* 97.2 (May 2015): 452–60.

5. See, for example, Gary Marcus, "Mice, Men, and Fate," *New Yorker*, May 13, 2013, http://www.newyorker.com/online/blogs/elements/2013/05/of-mice-and-men.html.

6. Alan Krueger, "The Rise and Consequences of Income Inequality in the United States," remarks prepared for delivery at the Center for American Progress, January 12, 2012, https://milescorak.files.wordpress.com/2012/01/34af5d01.pdf.

7. Robert H. Frank and Philip J. Cook, *The Winner-Take-All Society*, New York: Free Press, 1995.

8. Elizabeth Warren's 2012 campaign speech on debt crisis, fair taxation, http://elizabethwarrenwiki.org/factory-owner-speech/.

9. See Lant Pritchett, *Let Their People Come: Breaking the Gridlock on Global Labor Mobility*, Cambridge, MA: Center for Global Development, 2006.

10. Market Watch, "The Knot, the #1 Wedding Site, Releases 2014 Real Weddings Study Statistics," March 12, 2015, http://www.marketwatch.com/story/the-knot-the-1-wedding-site-releases-2014-real-weddings-study-statistics-2015-03-12.

11. Andrew M. Francis and Hugo M. Mialon, "A Diamond Is Forever and Other Fairy Tales: The Relationship between Wedding Expenses and Marriage Duration," Social Science Research Network, http://papers.ssrn.com/sol3/papers.cfm?abstract_id=2501480.

12. "Share Your DMV Horror Stories," http://www.early-retirement.org/forums/f27/share-your-dmv-horror-stories-27324-2.html.

CHAPTER 2: WHY SEEMINGLY TRIVIAL RANDOM EVENTS MATTER

1. Paul Lazarsfeld, "The American Soldier: An Expository Review," *Public Opinion Quarterly* 13.3 (1949): 377–404.

2. Duncan Watts, *Everything Is Obvious* (*Once You Know the Answer*), New York: Crown, 2011.

3. See Ian Leslie, "Why the Mona Lisa Stands Out," *Intelligent Life*, May/June, 2014, http://moreintelligentlife.com/content/ideas/ian-leslie/overexposed-works-art.

4. Watts, *Everything Is Obvious*, 59.

5. See Loren Kantor, "Casting Michael Corleone," *Splice Today*, April 1, 2013, http://splicetoday.com/moving-pictures/casting-michael-corleone.
6. Hollywood Reporter, "*Breaking Bad*: Two Surprising Actors Who Could Have Taken Bryan Cranston's Role," July 16, 2012, http://www.hollywood reporter.com/news/Breaking-bad-bryan-cranston-walter-white-amc -349840.
7. Robert K. Merton, "The Matthew Effect in Science," *Science* 159.3810 (1968): 56–63.
8. I was disappointed, but not surprised, when Ned left to join the University of Michigan faculty the following year. From there, he went on to various high policy positions in Washington. As a member of the Board of Governors of the Federal Reserve, he is most remembered for his sharply worded 2002 memo urging Fed chairman Alan Greenspan to take action against the strengthening housing bubble.
9. Watts summarizes the Music Lab experiment in detail in *Everything Is Obvious*.
10. Brett Martin, "Vince Gilligan: Kingpin of the Year 2013," *GQ*, November 13, 2013, http://www.gq.com/story/vince-gilligan-men-of-the-year -kingpin.
11. Malcom Gladwell, *Outliers*, New York: Pantheon, 2008.
12. Quoted by Gladwell, *Outliers*, 54, 55.
13. Leonard Mlodinow, *The Drunkard's Walk: How Randomness Rules Our Lives*, New York: Vintage, 1990, chap. 10.
14. Gavin Weightman, *The Frozen Water Trade*, New York: Hyperion, 2003.
15. Gladwell, *Outliers*, chap. 1.
16. Some authors have suggested that the success of players born earlier in the year results less from the fact that they are actually better than from the fact that NHL teams perceive them as better. See, for example, Robert O. Deaner, Aaron Lowen, and Stephen Cobley, "Born at the Wrong Time: Selection Bias in the NHL Draft," *PLOS One*, February 27, 2013, http:// journals.plos.org/plosone/article?id=10.1371/journal.pone.0057753. But even if this is true, Gladwell's claim still holds that an aspiring hockey star is lucky to have been born earlier in the year.
17. Elizabeth Dhuey and Stephen Lipscomb, "What Makes a Leader? Relative Age and High School Leadership," *Economics of Education Review* 27 (2008): 173–83.
18. Peter Kuhn and Catherine Weinberger, "Leadership Skills and Wages," *Journal of Labor Economics* 23.3 (July 2005): 395–436.
19. Qianqian Du, Huasheng Gaob, and Maurice D. Levi, "The Relative-Age Effect and Career Success: Evidence from Corporate CEOs," *Economics Letters* 117 (2012): 660–62.

20. Liran Einav and Leeat Yariv, "What's in a Surname? The Effects of Surname Initials on Academic Success," *Journal of Economic Perspectives* 20.1 (2006): 175–88.

CHAPTER 3: HOW WINNER-TAKE-ALL MARKETS MAGNIFY LUCK'S ROLE

1. Robert H. Frank and Philip J. Cook, *The Winner-Take-All Society*, New York: Free Press, 1995.
2. Sherwin Rosen, "The Economics of Superstars," *American Economic Review* 71 (December 1981): 845–58; quote p. 845.
3. Chris Anderson, *The Long Tail: Why the Future of Business Is Selling Less of More*, New York: Hyperion, 2006.
4. Anita Elberse, *Blockbusters: Hit-Making, Risk-Taking, and the Big Business of Entertainment*, New York: Henry Holt, 2013.
5. Barry Schwartz, *The Paradox of Choice: Why More Is Less*, New York: Harper Perennial, 2004.
6. The technological changes described by long-tail proponents enable you to make an informed judgment about the extent of my bias. You can review some of The Nepotist's music videos here: http://thenepotist.com/videos/.
7. Xavier Gabaix and Augustin Landier, "Why Has CEO Pay Increased So Much?" *Quarterly Journal of Economics* 123.1 (2008): 49–100.
8. Adam Smith, *The Wealth of Nations*, book 1, chap. 10.
9. The Conference Board, "Departing CEO Age and Tenure," June 13, 2014, https://www.conference-board.org/retrievefile.cfm?filename=TCB-CW-019.pdf&type=subsite.
10. Thomas Piketty, *Capital in the Twenty-First Century*, Cambridge, MA: Harvard University Press, 2013.

CHAPTER 4: WHY THE BIGGEST WINNERS ARE ALMOST ALWAYS LUCKY

1. High School Baseball Web, "Inside the Numbers," http://www.hsbaseballweb.com/inside_the_numbers.htm.
2. See *Wikipedia*, List of World Records in Athletics, http://en.wikipedia.org/wiki/List_of_world_records_in_athletics#Men and http://en.wikipedia.org/wiki/Athletics_record_progressions.
3. Because the probability of getting heads on each flip is 1/2, the probability of getting 20 heads in a row is $(1/2)^{20}$, which is 0.0000095367.

4. Carl Sagan, *Broca's Brain: Reflections on the Romance of Science*, New York: Random House, 1979, 61.
5. Chris McKittrick, "Bryan Cranston: 'Without Luck You Will Not Have a Successful Career,'" *Daily Actor*, October 31, 2012, http://www.dailyactor.com/tv/bryan-cranston-acting-luck/.

CHAPTER 5: WHY FALSE BELIEFS ABOUT LUCK AND TALENT PERSIST

1. Michael Mauboussin, *The Success Equation*, Cambridge, MA: Harvard Business Review Press, 2012.
2. Much of this research is elegantly summarized in Daniel Kahneman, *Thinking Fast and Slow*, New York: Farrar, Strauss, and Giroux, 2011. For an extremely readable account of how this work became important to economists, see Richard H. Thaler, *Misbehaving*, New York: W. W. Norton, 2015.
3. P. Cross, "Not Can but Will College Teachers Be Improved?," *New Directions for Higher Education* 17 (1977): 1–15.
4. Ezra W. Zuckerman and John T. Jost, "What Makes You Think You're So Popular? Self Evaluation Maintenance and the Subjective Side of the 'Friendship Paradox,'" *Social Psychology Quarterly* 64.3 (2001): 207–23.
5. College Board, *Student Descriptive Questionnaire*, Princeton, NJ: Educational Testing Service, 1976–77.
6. Richard Lustig, *Learn How to Increase Your Chances of Winning the Lottery*, Bloomington, IN: Authorhouse, 2010.
7. Charles T. Clotfelter and Philip J. Cook, "Lotteries in the Real World," *Journal of Risk and Uncertainty* 4 (1991): 227–32.
8. Nassim Nicholas Taleb, *Fooled by Randomness: The Hidden Role of Chance in Life and in the Markets*, London, TEXERE, 2001.
9. L. B. Alloy and L. Y. Abramson, "Judgment of Contingency in Depressed and Nondepressed Students: Sadder but Wiser?," *Journal of Experimental Psychology: General* 108 (1979): 441–85.
10. A. T. Beck, *Depression: Clinical, Experimental, and Theoretical Aspects*, New York: Harper and Row, 1967.
11. Alloy and Abramson, "Depressive Realism: Four Theoretical Perspectives," in L. B. Alloy, ed., *Cognitive Processes in Depression*, New York: Guilford, 1988: 223–65.
12. Underestimating the hassles of the job is of course equivalent to overestimating its attractions.
13. For a comprehensive discussion of this tendency, see George Ainslie, *Picoeconomics*, Cambridge: Cambridge University Press, 2001.

14. Roy F. Baumeister and John Tierney, *Willpower: Rediscovering the Greatest Human Strength*, New York: Penguin, 2011.
15. Roy Baumeister, quoted by Kirsten Weir, "The Power of Self-Control," *Monitor on Psychology* 43.1 (January 2012): 36.
16. K. Anders Ericsson, Ralf Krampe, and Clemens Tesch-Romer, "The Role of Deliberate Practice in the Acquisition of Expert Performance," *Psychological Review* 100.3 (1993): 363–406.
17. Attribution theory in psychology attempts to explain how people use information to arrive at causal explanations for events.
18. Bernard Weiner, *Achievement Motivation and Attribution Theory*, Morristown, NJ: General Learning Press, 1974.
19. Daniel H. Robinson, Janna Siegel, and Michael Shaughnessy, "An Interview with Bernard Weiner," *Educational Psychology Review* (June 1996): 165–74.
20. Jasmine M. Carey and Delroy Paulhus, "Worldview Implications of Believing in Free Will and/or Determinism: Politics, Morality, and Punitiveness," *Journal of Personality and Social Psychology* 81.2 (April 2013): 130–41.
21. R. F. Baumeister, E. A. Sparks, T. F. Stillman, and K. D. Vohs, "Free Will in Consumer Behavior: Self-Control, Ego Depletion, and Choice," *Journal of Consumer Psychology* 18 (2008): 4–13.
22. Thomas Gilovich, "Two Enemies of Gratitude," presentation at the Greater Good Gratitude Summit, June 7, 2014, https://www.youtube.com/watch?v =eLnAbkdXgCo.
23. Gilovich, "Two Enemies of Gratitude."
24. Thomas Gilovich and Shai Davidai, unpublished ms., 2015.
25. For an excellent survey of how views about luck differ along the political spectrum, see Dean M. Gromet, Kimberly A. Hartson, and David K. Sherman, "The Politics of Luck: Political Ideology and the Perceived Relationship between Luck and Success," *Journal of Experimental Social Psychology* 59 (2015): 40–46.

CHAPTER 6: THE BURDEN OF FALSE BELIEFS

1. American Society of Civil Engineers, Report Card for America's Infrastructure, 2013, http://www.infrastructurereportcard.org.
2. Donna M. Desrochers and Steven Hurlburt, "Trends in College Spending: 2001–2011; A Delta Data Update," Delta Cost Project: American Institutes for Research, 2014, www.deltacostproject.org/sites/default/files/products/ Delta%20Cost_Trends%20College%20Spending%202001–2011_071414 _rev.pdf.

3. Robert Hiltonsmith, "Pulling Up the Higher-Ed Ladder: Myth and Reality in the Crisis of College Affordability," www.demos.org/publication/pulling-higher-ed-ladder-myth-and-reality-crisis-college-affordability.

4. Phil Izzo, "Congratulations to Class of 2014, Most Indebted Ever," *Wall Street Journal*, May 16, 2014, http://blogs.wsj.com/numbers/congatulations-to-class-of-2014-the-most-indebted-ever-1368/.

5. Bruce Bartlett, "Are the Bush Tax Cuts the Root of Our Fiscal Problem?," *New York Times*, July 26, 2011, http://economix.blogs.nytimes.com/2011/07/26/are-the-bush-tax-cuts-the-root-of-our-fiscal-problem/.

6. Chunliang Feng, Yi Luo, Ruolei Gu, Lucas S Broster, Xueyi Shen, Tengxiang Tian, Yue-Jia Luo, Frank Krueger, "The Flexible Fairness: Equality, Earned Entitlement, and Self-Interest," *PLOS ONE* 8.9 (September 2013), http://www.plosone.org/article/info%3Adoi%2F10.1371%2Fjournal.pone.0073106.

7. Mechanical Turk, https://www.mturk.com/mturk/welcome.

8. John Locke, *Second Treatise on Civil Government*, 1689, chap. 5, section 27, http://www.constitution.org/jl/2ndtr05.htm.

9. Daniel Kahneman, Jack L. Knetsch, and Richard H. Thaler, "Anomalies: The Endowment Effect, Loss Aversion, and Status Quo Bias," *Journal of Economic Perspectives* 5.1 (1991): 193–206.

10. Liam Murphy and Thomas Nagel, *The Myth of Ownership*, New York: Oxford University Press, 2001.

11. David DeSteno, Monica Y. Bartlett, Jolie Baumann, Lisa A. Williams, and Leah Dickens, "Gratitude as Moral Sentiment: Emotion-Guided Cooperation in Economic Exchange," *Emotion* 10.2 (2010): 289–93.

12. Monica Bartlett and David DeSteno, "Gratitude and Prosocial Behavior: Helping When It Costs You," *Psychological Science* 17.4 (April 2006): 319–25.

13. M. Dickens, *My Father as I Recall Him*, Westminster, England: Roxburghe, 1897, 45.

14. Robert A. Emmons and Michael E. McCullough, "Counting Blessings versus Burdens: An Experimental Investigation of Gratitude and Subjective Well-Being in Daily Life," *Journal of Personality and Social Psychology* 84.2 (2003): 377–89.

15. Martin E. P. Seligman, Tracy A. Steen, Nansook Park, and Christopher Peterson, "Positive Psychology Progress: Empirical Validation of Interventions," http://www.ppc.sas.upenn.edu/articleseligman.pdf.

16. Nancy Digdon and Amy Koble, "Effects of Constructive Worry, Imagery Distraction, and Gratitude Interventions on Sleep Quality: A Pilot Trial," *Applied Psychology: Health and Well-Being* 3.2 (July 2011): 193–206.

17. C. Nathan DeWall, Nathaniel M. Lambert, Richard S. Pond Jr., Todd B. Kashdan, Frank D. Fincham, "A Grateful Heart Is a Nonviolent Heart:

Cross-Sectional, Experience Sampling, Longitudinal, and Experimental Evidence," *Social Psychological and Personality Science* 3.2 (March 2012): 232–40.

18. *Cityfile*, "Steve Schwarzman's $3 Mil. Birthday Bash: Any Regrets?" *Gawker*, October, 30, 2008, http://gawker.com/502741/steve-schwarzmans-3-mil-birthday-bash-any-regrets.

19. James Surowiecki, "Moaning Moguls," *New Yorker*, July 7, 2014, http://www.newyorker.com/talk/financial/2014/07/07/140707ta_talk_surowiecki.

20. *Slate*, http://www.slate.com/articles/business/it_seems_to_me/1997/05/herb_steins_unfamiliar_quotations.single.html.

21. Scott Clemens and Robert Barnes, "Support for Same-Sex Marriage at an All-Time High," *Washington Post*, April 23, 2015, https://www.washington post.com/politics/courts_law/poll-gay-marriage-support-at-record-high/2015/04/22/f6548332-e92a-11e4-aae1-d642717d8afa_story.html.

22. William Yardley, "Gustavo Archilla, an Inspiration for Gay Marriage, Dies at 96," *New York Times*, December 15, 2012, http://www.nytimes.com/2012/12/16/nyregion/gustavo-archilla-whose-wedding-inspired-gay-marriage-advocates-dies-at-96.html?_r=0.

23. On the volatility of social belief systems, see Timur Kuran, *Private Truths, Public Lies*, Cambridge, MA: Harvard University Press, 1995.

CHAPTER 7: WE'RE IN LUCK: A GOLDEN OPPORTUNITY

1. Market Watch, "The Knot, the #1 Wedding Site, Releases 2014 Real Weddings Study Statistics," March 12, 2015, http://www.marketwatch.com/story/the-knot-the-1-wedding-site-releases-2014-real-weddings-study-statistics-2015-03-12.

2. Andrew M. Francis and Hugo M. Mialon, "A Diamond Is Forever and Other Fairy Tales: The Relationship between Wedding Expenses and Marriage Duration," Social Science Research Network, http://papers.ssrn.com/sol3/papers.cfm?abstract_id=2501480.

3. Robert H. Frank, Adam Seth Levine, and Oege Dijk, "Expenditure Cascades," *Review of Behavioral Economics* 1.1–2 (2014): 55–73.

4. Samuel Bowles and Yongjin Park, "Emulation, Inequality, and Work Hours: Was Thorsten Veblen Right?," *Economic Journal* 115.507 (2005): F397–F412.

5. Robert H. Frank, *The Darwin Economy: Liberty, Competition, and the Common Good*, Princeton, NJ: Princeton University Press, 2011.

6. John Whitfield, "Libertarians with Antlers: What Robert H. Frank's *The Darwin Economy* Gets Wrong about Evolution," http://www.slate.com/

articles/health_and_science/science/2011/09/libertarians_with_antlers
.html.

7. To be sure, a trait might be wasteful from the collective perspective of males, yet still not be dysfunctional for the relevant species. As biologists have long noted, sexually reproducing species have far more males than they need, so if bull elk are more easily caught and killed by wolves because of their large antlers, that may not much threaten the survival of their species. But that wasn't my point. *The only claim I made on the basis of this example is that bulls would find survival to a ripe old age preferable to being killed and eaten prematurely.*

8. Robert H. Frank, "The Frame of Reference as a Public Good," *Economic Journal* 107 (November 1997): 1832–47.

9. Milton Friedman, "The Spendings Tax as a Wartime Fiscal Measure," *American Economic Review* 33.1, part 1 (March 1943): 50–62.

10. William Neikirk, "Bipartisan Sponsors Unveil Tax-revamp Plan," *Chicago Tribune*, April 29, 1995, http://articles.chicagotribune.com/1995-04-29/news/9504290130_1_tax-reform-plans-usa-tax-flat-tax.

11. Alan D. Viard and Robert Carroll, *Progressive Consumption Taxation: The X-Tax Revisited*, Washington, DC: AEI Press, 2012.

CHAPTER 8: BEING GRATEFUL

1. Italo Calvino, *Mr. Palomar*, London: Secker and Warburg, 1983, pp. 11, 12.

2. Ibid., p. 12.

3. O. B. Bodvarsson and W. A. Gibson, "Gratuities and Customer Appraisal of Service: Evidence from Minnesota Restaurants," *Journal of Socioeconomics* 23 (1994): 287–302.

4. Harvey Hornstein, *Cruelty and Kindness*, Englewood Cliffs, NJ: Prentice Hall, 1976.

5. See Robert H. Frank, *Passions within Reason: The Strategic Role of the Emotions*, New York: W. W. Norton, 1988, chap. 4.

6. Robert H. Frank, Thomas Gilovich, and Dennis Regan, "The Evolution of One-Shot Cooperation," *Ethology and Sociobiology* 14 (July 1993): 247–56.

7. Adam Smith, *The Wealth of Nations*, part 4, section 3, Library of Economics and Liberty, http://www.econlib.org/library/Smith/smWN.html.

8. Adam Satariano, Peter Burrows, and Brad Stone, "Scott Forstall, the Sorcerer's Apprentice at Apple," *Bloomberg Business*, October 12, 2011, http://www.bloomberg.com/bw/magazine/scott-forstall-the-sorcerers-apprentice-at-apple-10122011.html.

9. Jay Yarrow, "Tim Cook: Why I Fired Scott Forstall," *Business Insider*, December 6, 2012, http://www.businessinsider.com/tim-cook-why-i-fired-scott-forstall-2012–12.

10. Robert D. Putnam, *Our Kids: The American Dream in Crisis*, New York: Simon and Shuster, 2015.

11. M. A. Fox, B. A. Connolly, and T. D. Snyder, "Youth Indicators 2005: Trends in the Well-Being of American Youth," Washington, DC, US Department of Education, National Center for Education Statistics, table 21, http://nces.ed.gov/pubs2005/2005050.pdf.

12. Frank, *Passions within Reason*.

APPENDIX 1: DETAILED SIMULATION RESULTS FOR CHAPTER 4

1. My sincere thanks to Yuezhou Huo for her able assistance in carrying out the simulations in this appendix.

APPENDIX 2: FREQUENTLY ASKED QUESTIONS ABOUT THE PROGRESSIVE CONSUMPTION TAX

1. Robert H. Frank, "The Estate Tax: Efficient, Fair, and Misunderstood," *New York Times*, May 12, 2005, http://www.nytimes.com/2005/05/12/business/the-estate-tax-efficient-fair-and-misunderstood.html?_r=0.

2. "Buffett's Lasting Legacy: Immaterial Wealth," National Public Radio, May 6, 2010, http://www.npr.org/templates/story/story.php?storyId=126538348.

3. Alan D. Viard and Robert Carroll, *Progressive Consumption Taxation: The X-Tax Revisited*, Washington, DC: AEI Press, 2012.

INDEX

hostile takeover litigation, 36
human capital, 40, 66
Huo, Yuezhou, 95
Huxley, Aldous, vii

IBM, 34, 35, 51
Ice King, 37
income inequality, 52–55, 112, 113;
    and bankruptcy rates, 114, 115;
    and divorce rates, 114, 115; and
    government stimulus policy, 162,
    163; and hours worked, 115; and
    long commute times, 114, 115;
    and spending by the wealthy, 165
individual vs. collective incentives, 17,
    110, 117, 169
infrastructure, 12, 18, 87, 90, 91, 98,
    111, 119, 120, 124, 147, 162

jealousy, 122
Johnson, Harold, 134–41
Journal of Political Economy, 28
JVC, 44

Kahneman, Daniel, 28, 70
Kardashian, Kim, 9
keeping up with the Joneses, 112
Keillor, Garrison, 72
Kildall, Gary, 34–36
Koble, Amy, 102
Koufax, Sandy, 142
Kristof, Nicholas, xiv, xv
Krueger, Alan, 8

LaBelle, Patti, 103
Lake Wobegon Effect, 72
Landier, Augustin, 50
Langone, Kenneth, 104
last-name effects, 39
Lazarsfeld, Paul, 21
Leonard, Elmore, 5
Leslie, Ian, 22
Lewis, Michael, xii, xiii, xv, xvi
Liar's Poker, xiii
liberals, xi, 17, 83
Little League baseball, 142

Lockdown, 30
Locke, John, 96
Lokkins, Elmer, 106
London School of Economics, 4
Long Tail, The, 47
lost-envelope thought experiment, 130
lottery winners, 69, 72
Louvre, the, 22

Major League Baseball, 62, 141
Manove, Michael, 74
markets for classical music, 46, 47
Marshall, Alfred, 41
Martin, Brett, 31
material living standards, 14, 90
Matthew Effect, 24
Mauboussin, Michael, 69
McCullough, Michael, 102
Mechanical Turk, 95, 137
meritocracy, xi, xii
Merton, Robert K., 24
Mialon, Hugo, 14
Microsoft, 34, 35, 44
Milanovic, Branko, 7
Mlodinow, Leonard, 35
Mona Lisa, 9, 22–23
Morocco, 87
motivated cognition, 72
MS DOS, 35
Munger, Charlie, 39
Murphy, Liam, 97
Music Lab, 30, 45

Nagel, Thomas, 97
naïve optimism, 11, 12, 70–72, 75
National Center for Education
    Statistics, 87
National Institutes of Health, 135
natural selection, 73, 116
natural stupidity, 70
Nepal, 7, 14, 86, 112
Nepotist, The, 30, 49
Netflix, 47
Netherlands, 20
network effects, 43–45, 48
New Orleans, 25